"A very important work"

> — GEORGE D. KINDER, CFP
> Author of *The Seven Stages of Money Maturity*
> Founder of the Kinder Institute of Life Planning

"*Family Wealth—Keeping It in the Family* is a masterpiece. No one is more astute than Jay Hughes about the topics of family wealth and family life."

> — CHARLES W. COLLIER
> Senior Philanthropic Adviser, Harvard University

"Jay Hughes's reflections have dramatically changed the way exceptional families view their assets. His views on family governance, the family balance sheet, and control without ownership are essential reading for insightful families hoping to preserve their most important capital. Jay's contributions to the industry are immeasurable and much appreciated."

> — SARA S. HAMILTON
> Founder and CEO, Family Office Exchange, LLC

"'Those who do not learn from history are doomed to repeat it.' Jay Hughes, a passionate student of history, believes this more than most. His work with families, including his own, gave him the gift of learning the history of many, many families. Within that context he has written a book that illuminates previously only dimly lit concepts. For example, how can grandparents be the catalyst for the next generation's success? How should a family measure its own success as a family? Within IPI are many families indebted to Jay Hughes. He has shared with them the history of families and even more importantly, a blueprint for their own family's success."

> — CHARLOTTE B. BEYER
> Founder and CEO, Institute for Private Investors (IPI)

"This is the best book on family wealth preservation yet written. I would rate this book a '10' on a scale of 1 to 10. Jay Hughes helps people re-examine and redefine what their true family wealth is (hint: it's not money). Well if it's not the money, what is it, and how do you use the money to define, protect, and grow true family wealth for generations to come?

"That is the question Jay encourages families to explore and answer in this book. Regardless of your level of financial wealth, if you desire to use your resources to plant and grow a healthy family and create an environment from which its members can thrive on their own, this is a great book for you."

— Thomas C. Rogerson
   Senior Director of Wealth Management,
   Mellon Private Wealth Management

"Jay Hughes has taken his classic on family wealth to a new level of maturity and relevancy. It is a smart and sophisticated book offering both philosophical and practical insights on wealth stewardship. The sections on mentors, elders, and other key family members expand upon sage advice from the original edition.

"*Family Wealth* is a must read for family members, their advisers, and all those interested in deepening their understanding of how the affluent family can grow and sustain its most important asset— the human lives of the family and their connection to each other.

"*Family Wealth* is, as was true of the original edition, an impressive piece of work that is a foundational resource for wealthy families as well as the professionals of wealth consultation."

— Dr. Stephen Goldbart and Joan DiFuria
   Co-Directors, Money, Meaning, & Choices Institute

"Jay Hughes has given his distinguished career to the service of family legacy. He takes an approach to wealth preservation that values not only money but people. He shows us in *Family Wealth—Keeping It in the Family* why that approach matters and how it works for the family that wants a better future for itself and the world at large."

— PETER WHITE
Managing Director, Family Advisory Practice, Citigroup Private Bank

"All of us in the wealth management field have benefited by Jay Hughes's return to advising families on the responsibilities of having money. His unique background bridging law, religion, history, and philosophy provides a number of valuable anecdotes that are truly priceless lessons—not only for those who have money, but also for those who are servicing this sector in wealth management.

"*Family Wealth—Keeping It in the Family* is truly an ageless document that would have been as relevant in the 1820s as it will be in 2020. Mr. Hughes's writings and presentations have become the 'bible' in family governance and estate planning, spawning a number of disciples lecturing about his concepts of human, intellectual, and financial capital. We thank Mr. Hughes for his priceless gift of *Family Wealth*, which simplifies the understanding of the privilege of creating, inheriting, or owning money."

— TONY GUERNSEY
President, Wilmington Trust FSB New York

"Jay Hughes has been able to take his rich and extensive experience in the field of wealth preservation and distill it into an essential guide for the creation of legacy families. *Family Wealth* provides family members and their advisory teams invaluable direction as they develop a strategic plan for utilizing wealth for the purpose of creating generations of successful, productive families."

— LEE HAUSNER, PH.D.
Author of *Children of Paradise: Successful Parenting for Prosperous Families*
Partner of IFF Advisors, LLC

"In this book, Mr. Hughes literally brings to bear the wisdom of the ages in guiding the reader through the maze of stumbling blocks thwarting successful wealth preservation. His focus is healthy and holistic, centered on the preeminence of the family's human capital rather than the size of its coffers. As such, it is not a how-to book for those looking to hoard their wealth. To the contrary, this is an incredibly provocative, thoughtful (some might even say spiritual) guide. Its chapters light the pathway toward the responsible shepherding both of the people and the assets that, when properly aligned, make up a family's true 'wealth.' It is a must read for those we call patriarchs and matriarchs, their key intermediaries, all trustees and beneficiaries, and everyone who aspires to earn the title 'trusted adviser.'

"We who have dedicated our careers to the responsible use and constructive redeployment of wealth are privileged to have someone of Jay's caliber leading the way."

— MICHAEL J. A. SMITH
    Head of Wealth with Responsibility Program, U.S. Private
    Wealth Management, Deutsche Bank

Family Wealth

— Keeping It in the Family —

Family Wealth

— Keeping It in the Family —

How Family Members
and Their Advisers Preserve
Human, Intellectual, *and* Financial Assets
for Generations

Revised and Expanded Edition

James E. Hughes Jr.

Bloomberg PRESS

PRINCETON

This publication contains the author's opinions and is designed to provide accurate and authoritative information. It is sold with the understanding that the author, publisher, and Bloomberg L.P. are not engaged in rendering legal, accounting, investment-planning, or other professional advice. The reader should seek the services of a qualified professional for such advice; the authors, publisher, and Bloomberg L.P. cannot be held responsible for any loss incurred as a result of specific investments or planning decisions made by the reader.

Revised and Expanded Edition published 2004
1 3 5 7 9 10 8 6 4 2

Library of Congress Cataloging-in-Publication Data

Hughes, James E. Jr.
  Family wealth : keeping it in the family : how family members and their advisers preserve human, intellectual, and financial assets for generations / James E. Hughes, Jr. -- Rev. and expanded ed.
    p. cm.
Includes bibliographical references and index.
  ISBN 1-57660-151-X (alk. paper)
1. Estate planning--United States. 2. Finance, Personal--United States. 3. Family--Economic aspects--United States. I. Title.

KF750.Z9H827 2004
332.024'016'0973--dc22   2004001451

To my father, James E. Hughes Sr.,
an extraordinary adviser to families
and the wisest man I know;

to my mother, Elizabeth Sophie Buermann Hughes,
who first taught me about family
and who keeps creating family;

and to my partner in life and learning,
Jacqueline Merrill,
who put her arm through mine.

Contents

Part Three: Roles and Responsibilities

Part Four: Reflections

ACKNOWLEDGMENTS

Over the thirty-six years I have been journeying to learn the things I am sharing with you in this book, I have been mentored by many wonderful and extraordinary people. It is impossible to list each of you who have been of special help, and naming (in the case of my clients) you who have been my greatest teachers is unthinkable, as my honoring of your right to privacy is my greatest responsibility.

I would like to extend special thanks to my colleague Anne D'Andrea, without whose unfailing support this book could not have been written; to my typists, Rose Casella and Ann Cassella; to my wonderful office staff, Julianna Blunt, Linda Jackson, and Rita Jackson; to my readers of the original edition, Peter Karoff, John O'Neil, Sara Hamilton, and Joanie Bronfman; to my original publishers, Peter Hughes and Judith Arnold; and to William Lyons and Jared Kieling, who helped edit this revised edition.

My thanks also to Virginia and Juan Meyer, Suzan Peterfriend and Howard Shapiro, Ellen Perry, Rob Stein, Rosemary and Scott Reardon, Janet and Ed Miller, Henry Wyman, Ralph Wyman, Hap Perry, Peter Sperling, Robert Meyjes, Louis Dempsey, John King, Michael Smith, Richard Bakal, Christopher Brody, James Fordyce, Neen Hunt, John Stewart, Serge D'Araujo, Maria Elena Lagomasina, Terrence Todman, Tim Hawkins, Charles Vaughan-Johnson, Steven Hoch, Jim Jones, Ed Rudman, Patricia Meyer, James Deane, Walter Noel, Thomas Salmon, James Goodfellow, Florence Pratt, Patricia O'Neil, Nancy R. Hughes, Ellen Webster and John Webster, Nancy Elizabeth Hughes, Natalie Burton and Matthew Burton, Ned Rollhaus and Catherine Rollhaus, Alyssa Johl, Jennifer Fletcher, Roy Williams, John de Lande Long, Philip Lieberman, Kathy Wiseman, John Trask, Norman Wylie, Heidi Steiger, Francois de Visscher, Mary Lehman, Kate Aron, William Veale, Barry McCutchen, Patrick

Soares, David Horn, Mark Pollard, Kathryn McCarthy, Barry Geller, Sandra Lopez-Bird, Bente Strong, Tony Geurnsey, Lee Hausner, Daniel Garvey, Edward Bastian, James Ruddy, David Gage, Bryan Dunn, Michael Orr, Paul Setlakwe, Brian Rose, Dianne Neimann, Ellen Kratzer, Samuel Minzberg, Stephen Nelson, Hugh Freund, Kana Higashima, and Stephen Johnson.

Likewise, thanks to Warren Whitaker, Davidson T. Gordon, Chris Armstrong, Cliff Green, Charles Smith, John Layman, Nancy Lamb, Roberta Ruddy, Thomas C. Ragan, Jane Gregory Rubin, Mary Elizabeth Freeman, Mimi Hutton, Barry Wall, Joseph A. Field, Van Kirk Reeves, William Kriesel, Michael Pfeifer, Eugene Wadsworth, George R. Farnham, Emilio A. Dominianni, Agnes Anthony, D. Robert Drucker, Jr., Donald Kozusko, John Lahey, Richard Layman, Kenneth Hochman, Michael Horvitz, David Cowling, Anthony Stewart, Ben Fishburne, Chris Dugan, Richard Pogue, Richard E. Andersen, Barry Cass, Richard Guelph, Frank Wallis, Larry Brody, Robert Lawrence, Henry Zeigler, Edwin Matthews, Brian Fix, Ernst Stiefel, Jack J. T. Huang, David Morse, Walter Surrey, Mark Lebow, Gerald Dunworth, Hugh Fitzgerald, Gail Cohen, Marta Gucovsky, Peter Edwards, Edmund Granski, Jr., Ray Moore, Milo Coerper, David du Vivier, Charles Torem, Phillip Schreiber, Thomas Bissell, Dave Knudson, John Duncan, Rebecca Dent, Patricia M. Angus, Erin Stephen, Debra Treyze, George Harris, Nicola Jones, Anne Hargrave, Chester Weber, Brian McNally, Marna Broida, Bonnie Brown, Marilyn Mason, William J. Miller, Hill S. Snellings, Peter Evans, Art Black, Brett Barth, Evan Roth, Ulrich Burkhardt, Alex Von Erlach, Kenneth Polk, Spencer Sutton, Hunter Wilson, John Rhodes, Caroline Garnham, Richard Pease, Grant Stein, David Bird, Tim Ridley, John Campbell, Frank Mutch, Alec Anderson, Anton Duckworth.

Finally, to my son, William H. R. Hughes, my deep appreciation and thanks for the extensive editing he did to make this revised and updated edition come true. Working with him has been the best example of keeping it in the family I can imagine.

INTRODUCTION

Thank you for honoring me by opening this book and taking the journey it offers. To begin a journey is an act of courage. I hope your courage will be rewarded by new ideas and practices that will enable your family to preserve its wealth long into the future. To those of you (pilgrims on the road to Compostella) who read the first edition of *Family Wealth: Keeping It in the Family,* welcome back to the journey seven years later. I hope your journey so far has been rewarding and that your family governance systems are functioning well. I also hope you will find the ideas on elders, ritual, practices, evaluation of the third generation, mentorship, and the role of the *homme d'affaires,* newly included in this revised edition, a way to see what I have learned since we parted. To all who are journeying with me, let me paraphrase what Chaucer says at the beginning of the *Canterbury Tales:* As we are all pilgrims journeying to Canterbury individually, why not walk together and tell each other our stories? This is my story of family, and I welcome your stories as they join mine.

Thirteen years ago, I found myself professionally in the same "dark wood" described by Dante in the introduction to *The Inferno.* For the prior twenty-three years I had been honored by the decisions of many families to use my professional skills as an attorney. Most of these families sincerely believed that I helped them, and for many of those early years, I thought so, too. Gradually, however, I came to realize that while I was solving the problems they brought to me, most of these families were not successfully preserving their wealth when measured against the universal cultural proverb that we in America describe as "Shirtsleeves to shirtsleeves in three generations." I realized that the skills I had and, more important, my thought process in applying those skills, did not offer any solution to the proverb or, therefore, to my fundamental professional responsibility to these families. As this reality deepened its hold on me, I found myself in the "dark wood" wondering how, or even if, I should continue the active practice of law. Even more profoundly, I feared that I might be violating the most fundamental credo of any professional, "Do no harm."

After a period of retreat and reflection, I decided to begin exploring whether there was a way of thinking about the long-term preservation of a family's wealth, and whether there were practices a family could employ using that way of thinking, to overcome the effects of the proverb. I hoped that through this exploration I could continue to practice law using these ways of thinking and new skills to respond effectively first to the negative presumption of the proverb —that long-term wealth preservation by a family is impossible—and then to my individual concern that I should do no harm. This book is my effort to share with you what I have discovered so far.

To begin our process of discovery together, let me share some insights about myself so you know who you are journeying with and why I am so curious about this subject.

First, I am the great–grandson, on my maternal side, of a German immigrant who arrived in the United States during the Civil War. Soon after arriving at Newark, New Jersey, he enlisted as a "bounty soldier" in one of the New Jersey regiments. My great-grandfather did this because each bounty soldier received a substantial sum from another Northern boy who didn't want to take the risk of losing his life in the war. My great-grandfather elected to risk his life in order to have, if he survived, the necessary funds to start a business. Happily he did survive. (Otherwise, I wouldn't be here writing this book.) In fact, after a few years, he created what was for those times a substantial fortune. In terms of the shirtsleeves proverb, he was the prototypical first-generation creator of wealth.

My mother's father—my grandfather—was the ninth of eleven children. By the time of his maturity, the family was well-to-do, and all the executive positions in the family business were occupied by his older brothers. He discovered that he was free to pursue his own journey without the structure of work and financial responsibility required of his older siblings. During the Great Depression, he invested his part of his parents' fortune in a building in Newark. Unfortunately, his partner embezzled the firm's funds, and my grandfather went bankrupt. Thereafter, with very few useful skills and without the education about work that his older brothers had received, he was unable to provide adequately for his wife and three daughters. In my mother's family, we didn't have to wait for the third generation to lose our financial wealth—we lost it in the second generation.

This piece of family history has haunted me, because it seemed so unnecessary. It has been particularly difficult because my grandfather was my first real best friend. Without any doubt, my calling to the work of families and my efforts to help them preserve their wealth come in part from the history of financial wealth in my mother's family.

Second, on my paternal side, I am the sixth generation of my family to be involved with the practice of law. My great-great-great-grandfather was a justice of the peace in Virginia; my great-great-grandfather was a justice of the peace in Missouri; my great-grandfather was a district court judge in four counties of Missouri at the end of the nineteenth century; my grandfather earned a law degree from Washington University in St. Louis; and my father spent fifty years practicing law at Coudert Brothers, many of those years as one of its managing partners. My nephew, who works with me, is the seventh generation of our family to practice law.

This thread of my family history brings with it a very strict, almost Victorian, sense of a lawyer's responsibility to be just and to serve his client's interest in every possible way before considering his own. It also has meant that the practice of law is metaphorically, for me, the participation in a six-generation family business. The history of my father's family and its involvement in law has meant that I see my role as a lawyer both as a personal calling and as a responsibility to my forebears. It brings with it a passion to help people solve the problems they bring to me. This passion, I hope, developed not out of hubris, but out of a sense that this is my duty and raison d'être as a lawyer.

Third, I believe each of us learns in one of two fundamentally different ways, either through intensive study or intensive practice. I remain fascinated that the yogis of the Hindu faith understood and were applying this process of how we learn thousands of years ago. Then, and still today when a yogi accepts a new aspirant for spiritual learning, the yogi seeks to discover by which method the aspirant learns best. The yogi then applies this method to the aspirant's training. This fundamental divide in the ways we learn also means that to achieve complete understanding of any subject, we must balance our predilection to learn one way with an awareness of our lack of skill in learning by the second route. I learn most easily by the route of intense study, so I must work extra hard to learn by practice.

When I was in the "dark wood" and decided to begin the journey to try to find an answer to why families failed to disprove the shirtsleeves proverb, I set myself two tasks. First, I would educate myself, through reading, on every aspect of a family as a whole, on the relation of each member of a family to every other member, and on the spiritual underpinning of those relations as reflected in the world's major spiritual traditions. Second, I would ask the members of the families I was helping whether and how they practiced these relationships.

In 2000, I helped found a new learning institution (originally called the FOX Foundation, later The Learning Academy, and now called the Family Capital Institute) based on these Yogic learning principles with the added help of the work of Howard Gardner and Peter Vail. It has been thrilling to see family members learning together, in the ways each of them learns, the skills they need to successfully develop themselves and their abilities to participate in their family's governance systems.

The results of my study and my practice are reflected in the ideas and structure of the book.

Chapter 1 describes my philosophy:
- A family can successfully preserve its greatest wealth, that wealth being the individual human beings who form the family, over a long period of time.

- A family's wealth consists primarily of its human capital (defined as all the individuals who make up the family) and its intellectual capital (defined as everything that each individual family member knows), and secondarily of its financial capital.
- The purpose of a family is the enhancement of the individual pursuits of happiness of each of its members in the overall pursuit of the long-term preservation of the family as a whole.
- Successful long-term wealth preservation requires the creation and maintenance of a system of governance or joint decision making, to the end of making slightly more positive decisions than negative ones over a period of at least one hundred years.

Chapters 2 through 8 deal with practices that help a family define its mission, measure its success, learn to invest together, learn to enhance its members' financial skills and leverage their financial strengths, and best employ the skills of the families' closest advisers.

Chapters 9 through 15 explain a way of thinking about responsibility to the family as a whole, the mutual roles of beneficiaries and trustees, the role of family philanthropy, the role of external reviewers of the excellence of a family's practices (called peer review), and the possibility of creating a private trust company.

Chapters 16 through 21 contain further reflections on the roles of specific family members, mentors, and trustees, and a full discussion of the concept of a perpetual trust.

This book does *not* contain a chapter dealing with spirituality and its fundamental role in family wealth preservation. Every family I have observed that is successfully preserving its wealth is a reflection of the five virtues of truth, beauty, goodness, community, and compassion. Transcending all of these is its reflection of love. Families who preserve their wealth successfully reflect these virtues in their relationships both with family members *and* with all persons outside the family. I am convinced that without this spiritual component, a family cannot succeed in preserving itself, since its value system will fail and with that failure will come its disintegration.

Why, if this spiritual component is so fundamental, is it not discussed as part of my philosophy of wealth preservation in Chapter 1?

Because it is so basic that I am not sure a family can consider itself a functioning family if it is not already reflecting, expressing, and practicing these spiritual qualities. Second, I feel that my skills to help a family preserve its wealth can be successfully employed only by those families whose ethic includes these spiritual components when they first approach me for advice.

To begin a journey together for the purpose of enhancing the individual pursuit of happiness of each family member without the basic spiritual grounding for such a journey is to assure failure. Please always remember as you read this book that the ideas and practices expressed here are founded on my belief (learned from my mentor Peter White, who was the founder of International Skye and an early journeyer in this work) that these spiritual truths are the essential ethical fabric of your family. Without these spiritual truths underpinning your family's ethic, nothing I have written will make sense. If your family has not fully appreciated and incorporated this spiritual component into your unique ethic (your "differentness"), then start your family journey with a search for this spiritual component first, and then later use this book to help you when your family's journey has reached a point where it can incorporate and practice these ideas.

I hope that whether you learn best through the study of ideas (Chapters 1 and 16 through 21) or through practice (Chapters 2 through 15), you will find at least one suggestion within this book that will prompt you to have the courage to believe that the shirt-sleeve proverb can be overcome. *I believe it can!*

Family Wealth

— Keeping It in the Family —

PART ONE

My Philosophy

Chapter One

Long-Term Wealth Preservation as a Question of Family Governance

F AMILY WEALTH IS not self-perpetuating. Without careful planning and stewardship, a hard-earned fortune can easily be dissipated within a generation or two. The phenomenon of the fleeting family fortune is so well-recognized that it inspired a proverb: "Shirtsleeves to shirtsleeves in three generations." Vanishing wealth is not unique to the United States, and variations of this proverb are found around the world, from Asia to Ireland. The Irish variant—"Clogs to clogs in three generations"—depicts things in the following way. The first generation starts out wearing work clogs while digging in a potato field, receives no formal education, and, through very hard work, creates a fortune while maintaining a frugal lifestyle. The second generation attends university, wears fashionable clothes, has a mansion in town and an estate in the country, and eventually enters high society. The third generation's numerous members grow up in luxury, do little or no work, spend the money, and fate the fourth generation to find itself back in the potato field, doing manual labor. It is a classic three-stage process: first, a period of creativity; second, a period of stasis or maintenance of the status quo; and third, a period of dissipation.

Is this rags-to-riches-to-rags cycle inevitable? I believe it is not, and in this chapter, I outline my philosophy, describing why most families fail to preserve wealth over a long period of time; explaining

3

why this failure is unnecessary; and proposing a theory and method to practice successful wealth preservation. Below are the question, problem, theory, solution, and practice for how a family can preserve its wealth over a long period of time.

I. The Question: Can a family successfully preserve its wealth for more than one hundred years or for at least four generations?

II. The Problem: The history of long-term wealth preservation in families is a catalog of failures epitomized by the proverb "Shirtsleeves to shirtsleeves in three generations."

III. **The Theory**
  (A) Preservation of long-term family wealth is a question of human behavior.
  (B) Wealth preservation is a dynamic process of group activity, or governance, that must be successfully re-energized in each successive generation to overcome the threat of entropy.
  (C) The assets of a family are its individual members.
  (D) The wealth of a family consists of the human and intellectual capital of its members. A family's financial capital is a tool to support the growth of the family's human and intellectual capital.
  (E) To successfully preserve its wealth, a family must form a social compact among its members reflecting its shared values, and each successive generation must reaffirm and readopt that social compact.
  (F) To successfully preserve its wealth, a family must agree to create a system of representative governance through which it actively practices its values. Each successive generation must reaffirm its participation in that system of governance.
  (G) The mission of family governance must be the enhancement of the pursuit of happiness of each individual member. This will enhance the family as a whole and further the long-term preservation of the family's wealth: its human, intellectual, and financial capital.

IV. The Solution: A family can successfully preserve wealth for more than one hundred years if the system of representative governance it creates and practices is founded on a set of shared values that express that family's "differentness."

V. The Practice: Families should employ multiple quantitative and, more importantly, qualitative techniques to enable them, over a long period of time, to make slightly more positive than negative decisions regarding the employment of their human, intellectual, and financial capital.

I. The Question

Can a family successfully preserve its wealth for more than one hundred years or for at least four generations?

Allow me to summarize how I came to the discoveries and insights I am sharing with you. In 1967, I started my legal career in the trusts and estates department of Coudert Brothers. My father had then already been at Coudert Brothers for thirty-two years, specializing in corporate law. He continued to practice law at Coudert for another eighteen years. I had the good fortune to practice law with him during all those years and, most importantly, to be his student. His great interest was the succession issues of private and public businesses. He taught me that when businesses fail, it is most often due to poor long-term succession planning.

One of his favorite lessons came from his experience as a member of several boards of directors. When a new chief executive officer had been elected, my father said, "I would go up and shake the new CEO's hand and offer congratulations. He or she was naturally excited and feeling hugely successful since, in most cases, election as CEO represented the most significant event of the CEO's life and the culmination of years of very hard work. I would then immediately ask, 'Who is your successor?' There would be a look of surprise, and then, in the cases of the great CEOs, deflation, humility, and comprehension took the place of elation on their faces. After all, the most important role in the management of an enterprise is arranging for orderly succession."

My father's teaching has stayed with me. In every business with which I have been associated, whether public, private, philanthropic, or trust, the issue of succession has been critical to the long-term viability of that business.

My experience with families is exactly the same. A family's ability to remain in business over a long period of time always comes down to excellent long-term succession planning, regardless of how successful the family is financially.

Families attempting long-term wealth preservation often don't understand that they *are* businesses and that the techniques of long-term succession planning practiced by all other businesses are available to them as well. A family that starts its long-term wealth preservation planning by adopting the metaphor that it is a business will begin with a wonderful psychological tool. If a family thinks it is in business to enhance the lives of its individual family members, it discovers the most powerful form of preservation thinking it can do. The business metaphor further brings into a family's planning efforts all of the tools businesses use to be successful. As with all metaphors, one set of ideas created for a specific purpose cannot be perfectly suited to another purpose. The ideas can, however, offer a starting point for learning and for adaptation to the new set of issues being addressed.

Throughout this book, I will use the following terms.

- **Family:** Two or more individuals who, either because of bonds of affinity or because of genetic or emotional linkage, think of themselves as related to each other.
- **Wealth:** The human, intellectual, and financial capital of a family.
- **Preserve:** A dynamic effort requiring active employment of all elements of a family's human, intellectual, and financial capital in order to maintain the family.
- **Long-term:** A period of more than one hundred years, or four generations of the family.

II. The Problem

The history of long-term wealth preservation in families is a catalog of failures epitomized by the proverb "Shirtsleeves to shirtsleeves in three generations."

In 1974, I was asked by the sons of an enormously successful businessman in Singapore to come see their father. I was naturally curious about why I, a still very wet-behind-the-ears private-client attorney, was being invited to travel halfway round the world at substantial cost to the family when there must be excellent legal counsel available in Singapore. I suggested that I refer the businessman to someone local, but he was insistent, and so I accepted.

When the day of the meeting came, I still had no idea why I had been invited. After entering his enormous office and solving, over tea, all of the macroeconomic problems of the world, I was still wondering. Finally this worldly wise, enormously successful man said, "Mr. Hughes, you are probably wondering why I invited you here. We Chinese have a proverb, 'Rice paddy to rice paddy in three generations.' I don't want that to happen to my family. Can you help us using the techniques of families in America to solve this problem?" I was happy to discover that I could help him.

Through the years since 1974, as I have traveled to meet with families around the world, I have heard the same idea is expressed in varying ways. The shirtsleeves proverb turns out to be culturally universal, capturing a great truth about wealth and human behavior. Unfortunately, it describes only failure.

The shirtsleeves proverb describes a three-stage process: creation, stasis, and dissipation. Interestingly, this parallels the behavior of energy. As described by the laws of physics, energy comes together to form a new creation, undergoes a period of stasis or balance, and then moves by way of entropy or decay toward disorder. The energy, however, never disappears; it ultimately becomes part of a new creation, and the process begins again. Apparently all forms of life, which can be seen as organized forms of energy, must go through this cycle. The issue for families is whether they can extend the period of creativity through many generations, and thus postpone the periods of stasis and chaos for as long as possible.

A way I love to teach this lesson is to remind every generation of a family that it is the first generation. It has the same power of creativity as whichever generation was biologically the first. It is only when a family fails to perceive itself as the first generation that it begins to risk resembling the status quo of a second generation or the decay of a third.

What are some of the reasons this universal cultural proverb remains as true today as in the past?

First: In all cultures wealth preservation has meant, and continues to mean today, the accumulation of wealth measured as financial capital. Very few families have understood that their wealth consists of three forms of capital: human, intellectual, and financial. Even fewer families have understood that without active stewardship of their human and intellectual capital they cannot preserve their financial capital. In my opinion, the issue most critical to the failure of a family to preserve its wealth is concentration on the family's financial capital to the exclusion of its human and intellectual capital. A family's failure to understand what its wealth is and to manage that wealth successfully dooms that family to fulfill the shirtsleeves proverb. In fact, this concentration on financial capital may even cause it to go out of business in just one generation.

Second: Families fail to understand that wealth preservation is a dynamic, not a static, process and that each generation of the family must be a first generation—a wealth-creating generation.

Many family members who have inherited financial wealth have no concept of how difficult it is to create, and often their experience of the wealth creator was negative. These later-generation family members are rarely motivated by the same emotions that fueled the productivity of the originator of the initial family wealth. A family that imagines or, worse, assumes that every member of the family will be a wealth creator, or even that in every generation someone will have the creative instinct to be a great financial wealth creator, is fooling itself. Such a family is in entropy and will swiftly go out of business.

For a family to preserve wealth, it has to increase its wealth. How can it do this?

It can give greater thought to the preservation of the family's human and intellectual capital. It can understand its principal role as a dynamic one of creating new human and intellectual capital, while exercising excellence in its stewardship of the financial capital brought into being by the financial wealth creator. It is through such an understanding of each generation's principal role that every generation can, in practice, function as a new first generation of wealth creators.

Third: Families often fail to apply the appropriate time frames for successful wealth preservation. The result is that planning for the use of the family's human and intellectual capital is far too short-term and individual, and family goals for achievement are set far too low. Time should be measured by the generation. Otherwise, how can a family address whether it will still be in business in the fourth generation? Short-term for a family is twenty years, intermediate-term is fifty years, and long-term is one hundred years. With increasing life expectancy, I'm tempted to lengthen these periods, but for now they offer reasonable measuring sticks.

Almost every family I encounter is trying desperately to ensure that every year brings an increase to the bottom line of the financial balance sheet. I applaud this as an exercise in good financial stewardship. Unfortunately, though, if looked at over the twenty years of a short-term financial plan, these annual results simply become footnotes. In a fifty-year plan, they do not reach footnote status; they just appear on a bar graph. In a one-hundred-year plan, they are interesting only to the family historians.

An emphasis on short-term results is usually found cloaked in the mantra, "We are long-term investors." This unrealistic self-assessment frequently masks the fact that the risks necessary to achieve these annual goals—goals that even in a twenty-year cycle are extraordinarily short-term—are far too high in terms of the family's one-hundred-year financial wealth preservation plan.[1] When the twenty-, fifty-, and one-hundred-year terms of measurement are imposed on the family's investment strategy, the discipline of patience, which highlights the success of great investors like Philip Carret and Warren Buffett, shines forth. Patience is a virtue in everything a family does. For families setting their long-term strategies for preserving financial wealth, time is a friend in a way it is not for most investors. Equally, failure to take advantage of time is a waste of a valuable family asset.

When we move beyond the financial sphere and the family is measuring the preservation of its human and intellectual capital, its failure to understand the proper time frame for measuring success is even more profound. Some years ago, I was discussing the purchase of personal life insurance. I took the opportunity to ask my insurance agent about my life expectancy. I was delighted to hear him confirm that most of us are living longer than our grandparents or parents.

He told me that, barring a first heart attack or cancer before the age of fifty-five and assuming we do not smoke, the actuarial expectation for the large majority of us is that we will live well into our eighties and our children will live into their nineties.

For families in the wealth preservation business, this demographic information is fabulous news. Instead of losing individual family assets in their sixties, the family will get an extra twenty-five years' benefit out of the human and intellectual capital of the majority of its members. Any business that could extend the useful lives of its assets by twenty-five years would be in line for substantially increased profits. Every business knows that the cost of purchase of new assets is high, and keeping existing assets in excellent repair is critical to financial success.

In families, exactly the same business metaphor applies. When a family measures the useful lives of its members and plans for the maximum use of each member's human and intellectual capital over that member's lifetime, it defies the onset of the energy-depleting stages of status quo and entropy that are the greatest liabilities on its balance sheet. Failure to include the expected contribution and participation of each family member in the twenty-, fifty-, and one-hundred-year plan of a family is to have no plan for the management of the critical human and intellectual components of the family's wealth. Failing to measure properly fails to bring the newest members of the family into the family plan early enough to maximize their lifetime contributions. A business would never squander thirty years of the useful life of an asset. Failure to educate younger family members to a level at which they can participate and contribute to the family balance sheet is as much a waste of family assets as misjudging the useful lives of the oldest members of the family. The shirtsleeves proverb applies when families don't appreciate the power of twenty-, fifty-, and one-hundred-year time frames as a measurement of success in wealth preservation.

Fourth: Families fail to comprehend and manage the external and internal liabilities on their family balance sheets. Remember that the ultimate liability of a family business trying to preserve its wealth is finding itself in a blissful state of status quo, one in which nothing seems to be happening, supporting an assumption that there is nothing to worry about. In fact, what is developing is a state of decay, because liabilities were not managed properly in the earlier stages of the family's life. Chapter 4 discusses this subject in depth.

Fifth: Families fail to understand that the fundamental issues of wealth preservation are qualitative, not quantitative. Most families center their planning on quantitative goals. These families measure success based on the heft of their individual and collective financial balance sheets. Annually they add up their financial assets, subtract their financial liabilities, and determine their family's net worth. Individual members, and the family as a whole, also prepare detailed income statements showing the year's revenue minus expenses, and use that to determine that year's increase or decrease in the family's fortunes. This careful stewarding of balance sheets and income statements is critical to the management and preservation of the family's financial wealth. Unfortunately, this exercise doesn't take into account the family's qualitative balance sheets. The quantitative balance sheets have no place in their rows and columns to describe and evaluate human and intellectual capital and the annual increase and decrease thereof. Without a qualitative assessment of these two primary forms of capital, the family and individual balance sheets are incomplete and will not measure the extent to which a family is meeting its wealth preservation mission and goals.[2]

Four qualitative questions are critical to measuring whether a family is actively preserving its wealth:

• Is each individual member thriving?

• Is the social compact among the members of each family generation providing incentive to the leaders of each generation to stay in the family and listen to the individual issues of those they lead, so those members will choose to follow?

• Do the family members know *how* to leave the family wealth management business so they do not feel they *have* to leave? (This is in contrast to not knowing how to leave and then spending their lives trying to find out.)

• Are the selected representatives of the family meeting their responsibilities to manage the family's human, intellectual, and financial capital in order to achieve the individual pursuits of happiness of each of its members, and does each member perceive that they are doing so?

In later sections of this chapter, I discuss these four qualitative questions and why they represent the fundamental issues in successful family wealth preservation. Failure to measure the qualitative aspects of a family's preservation plan is failure to measure a family's most critical assets, its human and intellectual capital. Failure to understand and manage this reality leads immediately to entropy.

Sixth: Families fail to tell the family's stories. These stories are the glue that binds together the individual members of the family. Family stories give members a sense of the unique history and values they share, their "differentness." A family that does not inoculate its young against childhood diseases would be risking its most precious assets. Failure to inoculate the family's young against entropy with the vaccine of its history and the values that are contained in its stories is similarly risky.

Seventh: Families fail to understand that the preservation of family wealth over a long period of time is unbelievably hard work, work with a tremendous risk of failure balanced by a magnificent but distant reward.

Most of us know that a process, often a difficult one, is essential to the achievement of any endeavor. Most of us also know that abandoning the process too soon, because it seems too hard, is the most common reason that endeavors fail. Families who choose to enter the process of long-term wealth preservation face the daunting fact that their process will never end if they are successful. They have to decide to continue the process literally for all the generations to come. When I work with families who want to preserve their wealth, I explain this reality to them. To help them, and now you, decide whether to begin this process, I offer my favorite metaphor for family wealth preservation: the copper beech tree. If you don't know what a copper beech tree looks like and you want to see one, go to

Rhode Island and look in the front yards of many Newport mansions. When fully mature, a copper beech tree is the largest tree in the northeastern forest. It is a huge gray tree with a beautiful crown of copper-colored leaves that needs five or six adults, or ten children, holding hands to ring its trunk. Once mature, a copper beech tree will live for centuries.

Why is this beautiful tree my favorite metaphor for successful long-term wealth preservation by a family? First, think of the courage it takes to plant a tree that takes 150 years to mature. No one who plants the tree will ever see it full grown. Second, someone must invest love and patience to nurture it. Think of the hurricanes, ice and snow, pests, and fire that may consume the tree while it is too young to withstand those hazards. It needs help to survive these threats. Third, as it matures it has to contend with humans who want to cut it down for its wood, and with governments that want to put a road or a new housing development where it stands. The issues the growing tree faces parallel those in the unfolding life of a family. To complete this metaphor, here is a true story about the copper beech tree.

In the early nineteenth century, Marshal Lyautey, one of Napoleon's greatest generals, who was later buried alongside his former commander, was reported to have the most beautiful garden in France. Standing with his head gardener, looking out over his estate, he observed the wonderful specimens of the world's great trees planted there. Lyautey then turned to the gardener and said, "I see no copper beech tree." His gardener replied, "But, *mon général,* such a tree takes one hundred and fifty years to grow." Lyautey, without a second's hesitation, said, "Then we must plant today—we have no time to waste."

To embark on long-term wealth preservation is an act of extraordinary courage for a family, like the planting of a cooper beech tree, since the family members who initiate the process will never know whether they were ultimately successful. If you are courageous and you want to be a wealth creator in the most profound sense, get started. There is no time to waste.

III. The Theory

A) *Preservation of long-term family wealth is a question of human behavior.*

Most families whose cultural views are based on a modern interpretation of eighteenth-century Western European Enlightenment ideas believe that wealth preservation means successful management of their individual financial wealth. In part they are correct. But that emphasis leaves out the growth of their family's human and intellectual capital. It is the acts of family members, and not what they own, that is critical to success. Modern families also tend to think individually rather than collectively, and vertically rather than horizontally.

In many cultures of the world, especially Confucian ones like China's, preservation of the family is the main cultural preoccupation. These cultures know that family preservation is principally a matter of building the family's human and intellectual capital. They require all members to be educated to their maximum potential. They make decisions horizontally on what is best for the family, not just vertically on what is best for an individual and his or her immediate heirs. Chinese families act only after as many family members as possible have participated in the discussion. They understand that the growth of family financial capital is an effect of excellent management of their family's human and intellectual capital; it is not the cause. They understand, in other words, that human behavior determines whether a family preserves its wealth.

B) *Wealth preservation is a dynamic process of group activity, or governance, that must be successfully re-energized in each successive generation to overcome the threat of entropy.*

In an act repeated many times all over the world each day, two individuals elect to join their life journeys, and in this joint act they become a family. This joint act creates a system of governance and begins the process of wealth preservation in that family. Necessarily, the first steps in wealth preservation planning by this new family will be toddler steps. As time goes on, assuming the relationship of these two individuals survives, they discover that making one out of two is not as easy as their wonderful beginning romantic moments suggested. They discover that for their relationship to work they have to govern it well. For most couples their relationship leads to the birth or adoption of a child or children or, in cases where couples choose not to have children, to the nurturing of nieces and nephews. This next step in the creation of a family brings into the family's system of governance the first hint of long-term thinking. It is the moment when the long-term preservation of the family first becomes an issue. What happens from this moment on as the family begins the dynamic process of governing itself will determine whether one hundred years hence it is still thriving or has fallen into entropy and disappeared.

In this example, family governance begins with the creation of the family by the joint decision of two individuals to subordinate their individual freedoms of choice to a system of representative governance in which each has a role. This new government is highly energized at its beginning by the power of the two people who wanted it to be born and so gave it life. Very soon, however, it begins to subside into entropy as the romantic energy that created it begins to dissipate. The parties re-energize it with a new, more mature commitment to their original decision to be together. It is likely that, with this renewed commitment, the system of governance they organize will move the couple into a period of status quo, where they feel that their relationship works well and the governance system becomes the framework for their joint decision making. Normally, with the addition of children or nephews and nieces, the governance system will be re-energized again by the long-term planning that naturally arises with the advent of a new family generation. Unfortunately, in my experience, most families lose the new energy created by these new family members once the euphoria of their arrival is past and the reality of the responsibility of parenting takes over.

As the years go by, marriages, divorces, and deaths will occur. Each of these events will dynamically affect the energy of the family. As each new member joins the family, and as members leave, the governance system receives or loses energy. The capacity of the family governance system to acclimate to the ebbs and flows of energy is critical to successful wealth preservation. The life of a family is dynamic; the governance system it develops must be just as dynamic. The system must be able to use the positive energy pouring into the family with new members and to manage the loss of energy pouring out of the family with the loss of members. Management of fluxes in the family's human capital is the critical issue facing a family's governance system if the family is to successfully grow that human capital.

Every generation's renewal of the creative energy that brought two people together, expressed by the reaffirmation of the family's system of governance and the values that underlie it, is the creative process that will permit the long-term preservation of a family's wealth. Entropy or the dissipation of a family's creative energy is a family's ever-present foe. Reaffirmation of its creative energy is entropy's greatest enemy.

C) *The assets of a family are its individual members.*

Every family wealth preservation plan must begin and end with an acknowledgment that the most important assets a family has are its members. Businesspeople know that for a business to be successful, 70 to 80 percent of management's time must be spent on asset growth and 20 to 30 percent of its time on liabilities. My experience of almost every family is that they get this formula reversed. Any successful businessman who hears that a rival is spending 70 to 80 percent of his time on his liabilities knows that soon he will have one fewer competitor. Families who understand this spend 70 to 80 percent of their time growing their human assets. For example, they know that no matter how much they save in taxes, which are a cost or liability of doing business, those savings pale in comparison to the revenues lost through poorly educated family members. A family business that knows what its assets and liabilities are and apportions its governance time appropriately will find it is successfully preserving its wealth.

D) The wealth of a family consists of the human and intellectual capital of its members. A family's financial capital is a tool to support the growth of the family's human and intellectual capital.

The human capital of a family consists of the individuals who make up the family. The intellectual capital of a family is comprised of the knowledge gained through the life experiences of each family member, or what each family member knows. The financial capital of a family is the movable and immovable property it owns. A family must know whether all three of its forms of capital are growing.

Rarely in my experience do families measure their human and intellectual capital. Frequently, members do not even recognize that they own these forms of capital. Using my metaphor that families are businesses, can you imagine any enterprise being successful if it didn't track two of its three forms of capital? The managers of any business who could not tell its shareholders whether their capital was growing, or even worse, managers who didn't know what the business owned, would be summarily dismissed. The failure to acknowledge and measure the human and intellectual capitals of a family is a principal cause for the failure of a family to preserve its wealth. The positive acknowledgment by the family that it has three forms of capital, and the accurate measurement of all three, give the family and its shareholders a proper accounting of the state of its business.

When a family discovers that it has three forms of capital, it must then decide what its priorities should be for their management and use. Families who understand that the growth of their human capital is the first priority of their long-term wealth business have their priorities right. The physical and emotional well-being of the individual members of the family must be paramount. A successful determination that these individual assets of the family are thriving means that the most important of the family's forms of capital is growing.

With the growth of human capital must come the growth of a family's intellectual capital. In the information age, the strength of a family rests on what it knows. History likewise is full of stories of families succeeding because they knew something slightly before others and thus had more time to act on that knowledge than did their competitors. What is interesting is not that they had the good luck to gain the knowledge, but that they also were prepared intellectually to receive and to act on it when it came. Information is of no use unless you have a well-educated sense of how to discriminate in using it. In the modern era of instant communication, a family's ability to act intelligently on what it learns has become even more important, because the time available in which to take competitive advantage of opportunity has shortened.

I suggested in the Introduction that the successful practice of family governance will reward a family by causing it to make slightly more good decisions than bad over a long period of time. Given the ever increasing competition of other families for scarce resources, which will only get worse as the world's population grows, a family's ability to make excellent decisions becomes a more and more critical form of capital.

Directly measuring a family's intellectual capital is impossible, since no objective test could ever calculate exactly what every individual knows. The measurement of a family's intellectual capital must, therefore, be partly subjective. Family members' academic successes, career successes, artistic successes, and interpersonal successes are reflections of overall family intellectual capital. Another reflection of a family's intellectual capital is its growing financial capital.

To be sure, not every thriving member of a family will directly increase the family's financial capital. Individually, however, achieving one's highest intellectual and emotional capacity should enhance the family's overall capital in ways that will increase the family's financial capital, if in no other way than by making each person the best family shareholder, beneficiary, or representative he can be.

With growth of human and intellectual capital comes a high probability of growth of financial capital. Without growth of human and intellectual capital, financial capital may still grow, but it will not matter to the family's ability to preserve its wealth over the long term, since the family will go out of business as its human assets become less and less valuable.

Where, then, does financial capital fit in, if it alone cannot assure long-term wealth preservation?

A family's financial capital can provide a powerful tool with which to promote the growth of its human and intellectual capitals. After all, without human capital, there are no family assets; there is no family! Without intellectual capital, undereducated family members with all the money in the world will not make enough good decisions over a long period of time to outnumber their bad decisions. Successful long-term wealth preservation lies in understanding that it is the growth of a family's human and intellectual capital that determines its success, and that the growth of its financial capital provides a major tool for achieving this success.

E) To successfully preserve its wealth, a family must form a social compact among its members reflecting its shared values, and each successive generation must reaffirm and readopt that social compact.

There's a family in Europe, now in its tenth, eleventh, and twelfth generations, with many hundreds of members, that reaffirms and readopts its family constitution every year at a family meeting. The meeting takes place in the village where the family began. Although the meeting has an extended agenda, its acknowledged main purpose is to remind family members who they are, where they come from, and in what way they are "different." The family controls an extremely successful global business as well as substantial financial assets. Most members of the family lead comfortable lives financed by the earnings of the family assets. Very few work for the family, but all take their roles in selecting family representatives very seriously. All are educated about the family history and its constitution. When they reach their majority they join the earlier generations in the annual reaffirmation of the family constitution and in selecting representatives to carry out the system of family governance set out in the constitution. This family is succeeding superbly in wealth preservation.

This family demonstrates how a social compact among its members to govern themselves leads to successful family wealth preservation. The concept of a social compact as the foundation for a system of governance comes from John Locke's *Second Treatise of Government.* A social compact is an agreement among a group of people that expresses their values and goals and their voluntary decision to govern themselves according to those values and goals. A critical part of my theory is that the individual family members enter into a social compact, asserting their shared values and goals and their willingness to govern themselves according to those values and goals.

What does history teach us about social compacts and families? In earlier societies, particularly prehistoric ones, the recitation of the history of the society through stories was the glue that held the society together. It was through these stories that members of the society learned that they were different from other societies. It was through these stories that individuals learned who they were, and it was through their retelling of the stories that they reaffirmed their place in that society. These stories and their telling reflected these prehistoric societies' social compacts. In historic times, social compacts were reflected in the written laws of societies, in their religion, their myths, their art, and, in a macro sense, their cultures. Each individual who chose to remain in a culture understood his or her role, shared the culture's values, and, by participating in its rituals, entered into a social compact with the other members of that culture.

In modern times, written constitutions have become the repository of social compacts. The United States Constitution reflects, in its preamble, the shared values of the people who entered into its writing. These constitutional drafters understood that they were attempting to set up a system of governance that would reflect that set of values. Most importantly, they believed that the shared values expressed in the Constitution represented a compact among the American people upon which a government could be founded. The writers of the Constitution believed that without an underlying social compact among the individuals who would be governed by the new system, the system would fail.

As the Greek philosopher Aristotle reminds us in his book *The Politics*, families are the first and fundamental layer of all systems of government. It is in the family where individuals learn values. It is in the family where the first agreement or social compact comes into being through the giving up of some individual freedom in return for a perceived greater freedom.

One of the difficulties for families trying to govern themselves is that members tend to think of themselves mainly in vertical relation to one another. Each member measures his place in the family in relation to parents, grandparents, and great-grandparents. Family members rarely view themselves horizontally, in relation to siblings and cousins. Yet it is each generation, horizontally, that bears the critical duty of renewing the family's social compact if a family is to preserve its wealth over the long term. It is each generation of a family that must reconsider these shared family values and, if they are found still worthy of belief, reaffirm them. In families, I describe this reaffirmation process as "The Horizontal Social Compact."

I find it surprising that there is so little literature dealing with decision making between siblings or decision making between cousins.[3] The ability of siblings and cousins to learn to work together is critical to long-term wealth preservation. Every family I have studied that is still thriving in its fifth and later generations has, either through frequent oral recitation or written documents, committed to the memories of its members the family's shared values and the method of governance it uses to practice those values. Each of these families actively encourages each generation to reaffirm these values and practices. Each family encourages each later generation to form a new Horizontal Social Compact for its generation. If any generation fails to reaffirm the terms of the family's social compact, the ability of later generations to resurrect that compact as an expression of the family's shared values will at best be greatly diminished. Once entropy sets in through the loss of the family's social compact, it is nearly impossible, in my opinion, for a family to regain the capacity for long-term wealth preservation.

F) To successfully preserve its wealth, a family must agree to create a system of representative governance through which it actively practices its values. Each successive generation must reaffirm its participation in that system of governance.

Because a family is, by definition, two or more individuals, any decision made by a family must involve joint decision making. Joint decision making expresses a system of governance. Recognizing that joint decision making is a form of governance is one of the fundamental first steps in wealth preservation.

When a family recognizes that its decision making process is a form of governance, it also intuitively understands that by organizing itself to make joint decisions instead of individual and ad hoc decisions, it has a better chance at making more good decisions than bad. It has decided, as a joint endeavor, to organize the employment of its human and intellectual capital to make better decisions. In business terms, it is organizing its assets to obtain the maximum balance sheet power that comes from all of its assets working together.

Once a family understands that joint decision making is a form of governance, its next step is to choose the system of governance that will best serve the group of people who will be affected. To put it another way, the family must choose the system of governance that will cause the greatest number of family members affected to accept that decision as fair and to accept the individual consequences that flow from it.

Inevitably, conflicts arise when making family decisions that cannot be resolved within the executive body. A conflict dictates that a higher, impartial body must form the ultimate resolution. Regardless of a family's chosen system of governance, a judicial branch, or "Council of Elders,"[4] must be included to:

- effectively deal with internal family disputes;
- alert the family when they are not following the rules established in the family constitution; and
- render advisory opinions about how the family's values and goals inform the process of governing the family.

In my family's governance system, we have a family assembly consisting of my parents, my siblings, their spouses and significant others, and the eleven grandchildren and their spouses. We assemble annually to do the work of the legislative branch. On the infrequent occasions when a dispute arises among family members, these matters naturally flow up for decision to my parents, who may choose to include other members of the sibling generation in resolving the matter.

American families are blessed with the knowledge of how to form a representative government. Most of us learn how to make decisions together in the nursery with our siblings, in preschool, or in kindergarten. We are taught that joint decisions lead to better decisions. As children we learn that the United States of America came into being in the eighteenth century through two joint decisions, or social compacts, made by the then-voting population of America. (Unfortunately, this system did not yet include all Americans as voters; happily, it does today.) The agreements were written down by the men we call the Founding Fathers in the first of these social compacts, the Declaration of Independence, and later in the second, the Constitution and its first nine amendments, which we refer to today as the Bill of Rights.

Each of these documents states clearly that it expresses the values of Americans. Some of those values are that government should ensure each American the right to life, liberty, and the pursuit of happiness; that all people are created equal; and that the agreement itself represents a joint decision made by the American people, for the American people. We learn that a system of government is not just a set of rules; it is a set of rules that reflect deeply shared values. We learn that under the American system of governance, the people of America choose representatives to decide how the nation will make decisions to insure its long-term future.

In *The Politics,* Aristotle described the different kinds of governance he found in the world. Each system of governance described by Aristotle is still present somewhere in the world today. Remarkably, no new systems of governance have arisen since he wrote his book. Aristotle explains that the family is the first and smallest unit of governance. He further explains that the roles and practices of governance by families are reflected in the roles and practices of all larger systems of governance. In our modern parlance, the system of governance practiced in a family is a microcosm of all other systems of governance.

The systems of governance that Aristotle describes are an aristocracy, an oligarchy, a republic, a democracy (in modern terms an anarchy), and a tyranny (in modern terms a dictatorship). After discussing each form of government, Aristotle concludes that the system of governance called a republic is the best for human beings.

A republic is the form of government we refer to today as representative. This is a form of governance in which the people, whose social compact forms that government, elect from among themselves individuals to represent them. These individuals represent the people for an agreed period of time. At the end of the period of time, the representatives report back to the people on the outcome of their representations. If the people feel that the work the representatives were elected to do is not finished, the people may ask them to continue that work for a further term. If the people feel the work is finished, they may ask the same representatives to do new work. If the people feel the representatives did not perform their assignments well or that someone else is needed for a new responsibility, the voters will elect new individuals to represent them.

America's Founding Fathers, after studying the strengths and weaknesses of each possible system of governance, agreed with Aristotle, and so chose a republic as the system of governance for the United States of America.[5]

Every family I know, after it makes its own independent study of this subject, decides that a republic is the best system of family governance as well. These families discover that a republic best reflects the two principles of human behavior that a system of family governance must address in order to succeed.

The first principle is that human beings do not willingly give up some freedom unless they perceive that the reward for doing so is greater freedom. For example, a group where every individual carries a gun and feels free to use it represents anarchy, and no individual in that group is without fear. They are not free. Individuals in this example will willingly hand over their guns to a system of governance that will provide them individual security—real freedom. While all systems of governance are designed to provide order, only a republic provides a way for all of its members to participate in the selection of the representatives who will maintain that order. In this way they give up some freedom for what they correctly believe is greater freedom.

The second principle is that human beings do not willingly enter a group unless they believe they are free to change it or leave it. If human beings are unwillingly forced into a group, they will spend every moment of their lives seeking to leave it. A republic offers all family members the right to participate in the choice of family representatives. It also offers them the right to vote on changes in the system, and it offers them the freedom to leave without restraint if they no longer wish to participate. Aristocracies, oligarchies, and dictatorships prove this point by limiting participation in the process of choosing representatives either to a king or to themselves, and by limiting the ability of individuals to leave the system.

Families who study governance want to know why certain systems fail. Necessarily, they are particularly concerned about the future of the system of governance they have chosen. Polybius, a historian of the second century B.C. who wrote *The Rise of the Roman Empire,* describes how each of the systems of governance Aristotle describes decays into the next form of governance in a never-ending ordered process. He explains that the process begins with an aristocracy or kingship/queenship, which decays to an oligarchy, which in turn decays to a republic, which in turn decays to a democracy or anarchy, which in turn decays to a tyranny or dictatorship. Ultimately, the tyrant or dictator, anxious to form a dynasty to protect his or her family from events similar to those that brought him or her to power, moves from despotism to kingship or queenship and the cycle begins again.

A similar process occurs when a republic, where the voters elect their representatives and thus give up some individual freedom of choice on the outcome of a particular decision, decays to a democracy or modern anarchy, where each individual makes his own personal decision on the outcome of every decision. It is not the purpose of this book to discuss how each form of governance decays into another; Polybius has done that. I strongly recommend to families that they study this process of decay. If a family knows how and why a particular system of governance decays—that is, goes into entropy—it will have a historically proven method to measure how its chosen system of family governance is currently performing against its particular nemesis. Families who study and use Aristotle and Polybius are drawing on the same historical sources as the Founding Fathers. They are choosing the governance system that best represents their now educated views on how to organize themselves to best reflect their values and to increase the probability that their joint decisions will be good ones. They have understood that the critical first step for a family beginning long-term wealth preservation is to found an excellent system for decision making, a system of governance.

The second step is adoption of a formal process for each successive generation to reaffirm its acceptance of the family's system of governance. Just choosing a good system of governance does not mean a family will successfully preserve its wealth over a long period of time. For a system of governance to provide a means for excellent joint decision-making over the long term, family members must develop a belief in the inviolability of the chosen system, transcending the choices of process of governance that any particular generation might otherwise make. The system of governance must become the expression of the family's value system, its differentness, rather than the expression of the views of its founders alone.

As an example, when the Constitution of the United States was adopted, many people in America were opposed to it and the republican system of governance it represented. Some Americans wanted a monarchy or an aristocracy. Some wanted an oligarchy, and some wanted a pure democracy, or anarchy. No American wanted a tyranny or dictatorship. When Americans were choosing their system of governance, any one of these systems might have been adopted. Ultimately, after a countrywide debate, the written Constitution reflected the choice of the majority of voters that a republic was the correct form of governance for the United States of America. Today very few Americans think about whether we should change our system of governance to an aristocracy, oligarchy, or anarchy. Americans are united in their belief in the Constitution and the system of governance it represents.

Americans have gone to war to protect the values the Constitution represents. Their belief in the Constitution, as representation of them as Americans, has transcended what otherwise might be their individual views on the best system of governance. Americans now think of themselves as "American" by identifying with the values expressed by the Constitution.

For any system of governance to provide a means for excellent decision making over a long period of time, it must be inculcated into the belief systems of every member of the family in every generation. The system must come to be seen as the foundation for each individual member's success and for the family's overall success. A part of this process of transcendence is the constant reaffirmation by family members of the values expressed by the governance system. Without reaffirmation, the system will gradually lose its vitality and at best become a cherished relic of family history. To be useful, a system of governance must be a dynamic, vital system for current decision making. Each successive family generation, by its affirmative decision to be governed by the chosen system, revitalizes the system. In our American system, this process of revitalization occurs every two years with elections. The framers of the Constitution knew that the social compact represented in the document could not be sustained unless this compact was renewed frequently through elections. This same principle of renewal is just as critical to the success of a family system of governance.

The third step in achieving a successful system of family governance is the adoption of a process to amend its practices as the family evolves. A governance system necessarily reflects the particular issues that caused the people who created it to bring it into being. No matter how well designed, such a system can never foresee all the issues that the people who live under it will need to manage in the future. New individual and family issues will quickly arise. A system of governance must have the flexibility to provide excellent solutions to the problems posed by such new issues. Flexibility, however, also poses dangers. If the system can be changed too easily, it will quickly break down as each new issue leads to a debate on the utility of the system itself.

As an example, the Constitution contains a process for its own amendment. The framers recognized that the system needed to be flexible enough to address future issues they could not foresee. They also recognized the danger of a system that could easily be changed. The framers, therefore, decided to make it very difficult, but not impossible, to change the fundamental rules that voters originally adopted. This wise decision is, in my opinion, the single most important reason why the American Constitution has worked so well for more than 200 years. The individuals who live under the Constitution revere its basic principles. They revere these principles not because they are perfect, but because they have proven their excellence through their successful applications to ever-changing issues. Only on the rare occasions when an issue could not be resolved by these principles were the founding principles modified.

In many other countries that have adopted the republic form of government, the constitutional experience has been less successful. I believe the primary reason for this lack of success is the ease with which these countries' constitutions can be amended. How can people believe in the transcendence of a system of governance if it can be changed by a simple majority of representatives every time a new issue arises? Gradually the changes will be so numerous that they will overwhelm the original founding principles. Instead of shared fundamental values, the constitution will reflect individual answers to specific historical issues. This represents decay of the constitution and the system of governance it was created to represent. Ultimately this constitution will fail and will have to be replaced, attended by all of the changes to the society this represents. The French and the Italian experiences with constitutions are sad examples of this reality.

New issues in families, as in all other groups, will trigger a reconsideration of values and the system of family governance, and this is as it should be. To be effective, a family system of governance must include the possibility of amendment to meet issues posed by the family's evolution. To be effective over a long period of time, however, the system also must recognize that amendment, as in the American system, should occur only if there is a compelling need to change a fundamental value. Amendments must not be seen as an appropriate way to deal with issues of today that may disappear tomorrow.

The final step in achieving excellent family governance is the adoption of a formal set of checks and balances to ensure that family members control the process of governance. In later chapters of this book, I discuss how representatives are held accountable to a standard of excellence. In those chapters I explain that successful long-term wealth preservation occurs when each family member actively carries out her or his function of being a person to whom each family representative is accountable.

If a family selects the republic as its model, it must build into its governance system checks and balances similar to those placed on the American executive, legislative, and judicial branches. In a family republic, the individual family members are the voters. In a diagram of the system of governance, the names of all the family's members should be placed at the top, not at the bottom. A family system of governance fails if each member does not understand that the individuals and corporations selected to carry out tasks for the family directly represent him or her as a voter. A family system of governance succeeds through the willingness of each member to participate fully in the selection of excellent representatives and in holding those representatives accountable for the excellence of their representation. If representatives believe that the people they represent really care about excellence, they will strive to be excellent. Apathy or outright indifference by family members to the excellence of the representatives selected and to participation in their selection leads to stagnation and ultimately to failure of governance. Successful family governance requires all family members to dynamically exercise their roles as voters, as the persons being represented, and as the persons to whom the family representatives are accountable.

G) *The mission of family governance must be the enhancement of the pursuit of happiness of each individual member.* This will enhance the family as a whole and further the long-term preservation of the family's wealth: its human, intellectual, and financial capital.[6]

Many years ago at the Far Brook School in New Jersey, it was my privilege to have been taught American history by an extraordinary teacher, Ara Dodds. Mrs. Dodds explained to my class that the American Declaration of Independence said that every American was entitled to a system of governance that worked to ensure his right to life, liberty, and the pursuit of happiness. As a boy I could understand life and liberty, but the pursuit of happiness sounded very strange. I knew it didn't mean being happy in a silly way, since I knew Thomas Jefferson was serious about the meaning of every word in the Declaration. I couldn't imagine that people would go to war risking their lives and property over a frivolous idea. A few years ago I read Aristotle's *Nichomachean Ethics* for the first time. In the book, Aristotle explains that all lives of virtue are lived in the pursuit of an individual's happiness. I discovered, as so many others have, that Jefferson lifted his famous phrase from Aristotle.

Thus did Aristotle's view of a virtuous life and its process, the pursuit of happiness, find new expression in the foundation of American governance. Aristotle, being a grizzled veteran of the Greek political wars, knew that to lead a virtuous life was very difficult. He defined virtuousness, and I paraphrase, as being just, brave, temperate, and moderate in all things. These are hard things to achieve. He also said, and again I paraphrase, that you did not know whether you had led a virtuous life and thus pursued happiness until the day after you died—another very tough test of an individual's constancy.

Other philosophers since Aristotle have offered their views on the same subject, usually varying the ingredients of virtue but never changing the fundamental idea that life is a journey in pursuit of the happiness for which each of us searches. A modern philosopher, the mythographer Joseph Campbell, expressed his view of the journey in pursuit of happiness as "follow your bliss." I believe that Aristotle in the fourth century B.C. and Thomas Jefferson in the eighteenth century were correct in considering the primary mission of governance at any level to be the enhancement of the pursuit of happiness of the governed.

Once a system of family governance accepts as its mission the enhancement of the pursuits of happiness of its individual members, it discovers a second level to its mission: the enhancement of the whole that evolves naturally out of the enhancement of its parts. A family is an ever-changing mosaic of individuals. When each individual is successfully pursuing her or his happiness, the colors of the whole mosaic are vibrant, and there are no blank spaces that spoil the picture. A dull mosaic, or one with blank spaces, is a reflection of deterioration and entropy. A successful family system of governance enhances the family as a whole by enhancing the pursuit of happiness of each members.

The third level of the mission of a family governance system is to promote the long-term growth of the family's wealth: its human, intellectual, and financial capital. In this dimension of its mission, the governance system oversees the "family business." Family members set the mission of the enterprise, develop policies for the growth of the family's capital, and choose the family's executive body, the equivalent of its board of directors, to manage those policies. The executive body in turn chooses family executives—family office management and trustees; advisers, mentors, and protectors; and peer reviewers—to carry out those policies.

A successful family governance system produces a three-dimensional structure—members, directors, and executives—within which all three levels of mission can be managed at the same time.

IV. The Solution

A family can successfully preserve wealth for more than one hundred years if the system of representative governance it creates and practices is founded on a set of shared values that express that family's differentness.

My theory is that families can successfully overcome the "Shirtsleeves to shirtsleeves in three generations" proverb. As proof, I offer the following examples of families that have prospered over several generations. None of these families are clients of mine, nor have I asked them for permission to discuss their histories. I also have no idea whether they would agree with the observations I am making about them. Everything I relate about them is based on public information I discovered by reading and by attending open professional meetings.

My first example is the Rothschilds. In the mid-eighteenth century, Mayer Amschel Rothschild founded the House of Rothschild. This creator of the Rothschild fortune had five sons, each of whom he set up in the banking business in one of the era's five principal European financial capitals: Frankfurt, Vienna, London, Paris, and Naples. He lent them the money to get started with the proviso that they pay him back so that the "family bank" could make further loans to family members. He directed that each son could keep the profits of his individual bank once the original loan had been repaid. He charged interest on the loans at a lower than normal rate. He also charged interest in the form of intellectual currency. He requested each of his sons relay to him every bit of financial information he gained in his city. He agreed to share this intellectual interest with his other sons. In modern terms, he created an effective information network.

Mayer Amschel Rothschild also used a powerful investment technique to manage the risk to his family's human capital. By sending each son to a different city, he diversified his human assets into five separate investments, thereby increasing the probability that at least one of the branches would survive political and economic risks. History shows how farsighted his geographic diversification strategy was. The branches of the family business in Frankfurt, Vienna, and Naples failed because of historical events. The London and Paris branches survived and continue to prosper. Had Mayer Amschel Rothschild kept all of his sons in Frankfurt, where he started his business, and not diversified the risks to his human capital, it is unlikely any part of his business would have survived the Holocaust. Diversity also increased the family's intellectual capital by giving each son his own opportunity to prosper or, in my terms, to pursue his happiness. Today, some 250 years later, the name Rothschild is synonymous with wealth.

What are the lessons we can learn from this remarkable family's ability to overcome the shirtsleeve proverb? First, Mayer Amschel Rothschild understood that one form of a family's wealth is its human capital. With five sons and their progeny, he was able to found a dynasty. Additionally, he saw to it that they were all well educated and that they worked. Second, Mayer Amschel Rothschild understood that a family has intellectual capital. His brilliant use of that capital, including his idea for the payment and circulation of "intellectual interest" in the form of information gleaned by his sons as they carried on their respective banking businesses, was crucial to the Rothschild success. It quickly made them leaders in their profession and earned them great wealth. Information then and now is the most valuable contributor to wealth creation and preservation. A family without intellectual capital can receive the most timely financial information but be unable to do anything with it.

Third, Mayer Amschel Rothschild understood the use of financial capital in long-term wealth preservation, as he demonstrated by lending, rather than giving, money to his sons. By lending the money and being repaid he could re-circulate his capital to the best business opportunities throughout Europe. He was also able to teach his sons what life was like for their business competitors who were not lucky enough to have a wealthy father. His lending practices led to growth in the family's financial capital and, more importantly, to growth of the family's intellectual capital.

Before finishing the Rothschild story I must note the family's extraordinary philanthropic generosity. The Rothschild family is legendary in Europe for its good citizenship and its concern for others. In Chapter 12, "Family Philanthropy," I discuss the human and intellectual capital growth a family achieves through philanthropy. Families learn more about long-term wealth preservation through giving than they do through spending or accumulating. Values discussions grow easily out of giving to others, and positive and successful mission statements grow out of values discussions.

Finally and most importantly, Mayer Amschel Rothschild created a system of family governance that succeeded in preserving the family's wealth. Many external liabilities beset the Rothschilds, such as the horrors of the European wars (especially the Holocaust), death, divorce, taxation, Malthus's Law, and inflation. The Rothschild family, albeit affected by these liabilities, is still progressing and still governing itself well. To be a Rothschild 250 years after the founding of the House of Rothschild is to be a member of a very successful family, one that continues to preserve its human, intellectual, and financial capital.

My second example is the Rockefellers. In the mid-nineteenth century, John Davison Rockefeller, Sr., founded the Rockefeller family fortune. Thanks to his business acumen, diligence, and long life, Rockefeller had amassed America's largest fortune by the time of his death, at age ninety-eight. He was also a great philanthropist, and as with the Rothschilds, philanthropy continues to play a significant part in the successful long-term wealth preservation planning of the Rockefeller family.

John Davison Rockefeller, Sr., had one son, John D. Rockefeller, Jr. His son decided at an early age that he was not interested in a business career and, with the agreement of his father, devoted the rest of his life to family governance and philanthropy. John D. Rockefeller, Jr., was as superb a creator of family as his father was of business, and he was an even more successful philanthropist. John D. Rockefeller, Jr., had six children—one daughter and five sons. To this third generation, he bequeathed a system of family governance that continues today to grow the long-term wealth of the Rockefeller family's fourth, fifth, and sixth generations.

John D. Rockefeller, Jr., set up a family office to serve the wealth management needs of each family member who chose to use its services. While the office prides itself on excellent investment performance, its greatest value to the family is its wealth of educational services in finance and philanthropy. The family office's principal mission is to grow the human and intellectual capital of the family. John D. Rockefeller, Jr., instituted the concept of annual family meetings. Today, all Rockefeller family members are invited to meet once a year at the family seat. The agenda includes individual concerns, generational concerns, and familywide concerns. The Rockefeller vision—that each generation has issues unique to it and that it must deal with—is brilliant. In every system of family governance a critical part of the system's long-term viability is the reaffirmation of its vitality by each generation, as it comes of age, through its willingness to actively participate. The regular discussion of generational issues is a critical part of the success of the Rockefeller system of governance. John D. Rockefeller, Jr., also developed many excellent practices with respect to the role of family members as employees of the family, the role of outside board members and advisers, and the practices of philanthropy. These have become "best practices" in many other family governance structures.

An unrecognized part of the Rockefeller's success in long-term wealth preservation is the extraordinary act by John Davison Rockefeller, Sr., of not compelling his son to remain in the family business once he had determined that his calling lay in family governance and philanthropy. Here is America's wealthiest man, with only one son, agreeing that the son was not obliged to follow the father's dreams. I believe the father's willingness to free his son to follow his individual pursuit of happiness is one of the best long-term wealth preservation decisions in history. It is interesting that John Davison Rockefeller, Sr., continued for the rest of his life to do what he loved, thereby adding immeasurably to the family's intellectual and financial capital. It is also interesting that John D. Rockefeller, Jr., urged each of his children to find work that led to their individual pursuits of happiness. The resulting contributions of the third-generation Rockefellers to philanthropy, government, international banking, and investment in new industries are remarkable. Today, more than 120 years since the founding of the fortune, the Rockefeller family clearly understands that its wealth lies in its human and intellectual capital, and that its financial capital is a tool to enhance the pursuits of happiness of its individual members.

Other well-known families who have overcome the shirtsleeves proverb are the Mitsubishis in Japan, the Soongs in China, the Tatas and Birlas in India, the Windsors and Westminsters in the United Kingdom, and the Krupps in Germany.

Although proverbs about the fleeting nature of family fortunes are found in every culture on the globe, there are families around the globe who are defeating it. The failure of a family to preserve its wealth for more than three generations is not predestined. The exercise by a family of its free will to successfully combat and overcome the dictum of the shirtsleeves proverb is an ever-present possibility.

V. The Practice

Families should employ multiple quantitative and, more importantly, qualitative techniques to enable them, over a long period of time, to make slightly more positive than negative decisions regarding the employment of their human, intellectual, and financial capital.

Wealth preservation is a dynamic process. Any family whose wealth of human, intellectual, and financial capital is simply maintaining value rather than growing is either in or in danger of entering a state of decay or entropy. A family, like every investor, must maximize its return on capital if it is to achieve the growth necessary for preservation over a long period of time. What are some of the things a family can do to maximize the return on its human, intellectual, and financial capital?

With respect to its human capital, a family should implement the following ideas:

1) It must stretch the physical capacities of each family member to achieve each member's maximum well-being. This includes providing the best possible medical care to every family member whose pursuit of happiness is blocked by addiction or physical or mental illness.

2) It must ensure that every family member's basic requirements for food, shelter, and clothing are met, and for members who experience a life emergency, that those needs are met at a level adequate to allow them to regain the capacity for the pursuit of individual happiness.

3) It must ensure that every family member understands, at the highest educational limit possible for that member, the workings of the family governance system and her or his role in it.

4) It must emphasize the importance of the dignity of work to an individual's sense of self-worth and assist each family member in finding the work that most enhances that individual's pursuit of happiness. All such work is of equal value to the growth of the family's human capital, regardless of its financial reward.

5) It must encourage the geographic diversification of human assets. The world is becoming smaller every day. Families must participate in all corners of the world if they are to meet the challenges of a global world.

6) It must encourage the recognition and practice of the family's spiritual values as expressed in the family mission statement, its system of governance, and its philanthropy.

With respect to its intellectual capital, a family should implement the following ideas:

1) It must provide a means for the collection and dissemination of the accumulated knowledge of all family members.

2) It must rapidly provide clear information on all family governance matters to all family members at the highest level of each individual's ability to understand and seek feedback.

3) It must provide incentives for the family's highest achievers to take representative and leadership roles within the family governance structure.

4) It must provide tools to younger members to learn the family stories and prepare for later roles in family governance.

5) It must strive to develop in each family member the seven intelligences that Howard Gardner defines in his book, *Frames of Mind*. A family's members comprise many abilities, and each is critical to the growth of its intellectual capital.

6) It must stretch the intellectual capacity of each member to achieve each member's maximum level of learning.

7) It must diversify its intellectual capital by encouraging its members to study all of the world's cultures and languages. The world is growing ever smaller with modern communications, and relevant opportunities now occur all over the world. Families of the twenty-first century, like the Rothschilds of the eighteenth, must diversify their intellectual capital to encompass every niche of the world's learning in order to overcome competition.

With respect to its financial capital, a family must remember above all to measure its growth over twenty-, fifty-, and one-hundred-year periods, and to take risks commensurate with such long-term planning periods.

While the practice of these and other techniques in the book will not guarantee that a family will preserve its wealth for a long period of time, they will provide a family with helpful tools for making slightly more good decisions than bad. Any novice investor learns about the power of compounding. A family whose wealth preservation system leads it to make slightly more wealth-preserving decisions than non-preserving decisions will tap into that same power of compounding.

One theory about the life of the universe is that the universe is growing just slightly more than is needed to overcome stasis and its more assertive companion, entropy. That theory suggests that the life of the universe could be perpetual. The universe, like all other dynamic systems, must manage the risks that are inherent in the conditions of its existence, and all of us know that to overcome risk you have to take risk. Excellent investors know how to take just enough risk, and no more, to achieve their investment goals. They are never rash, they exercise patience, and they seek the solid gains that come from compounding the rewards of their patient risk taking. If the universe can achieve long-term preservation by growing slightly more than is needed to overcome stasis, why shouldn't a family follow the same logic to preserve its wealth?

Chapter Notes

1. Don't worry; I am aware of inflation, Malthus's Law, and taxes. I'll discuss them later.

2. In Chapter 4, "The Family Balance Sheet and Family Income Statement," I explain how a qualitative balance sheet is constructed and what it measures.

3. An exception is the work on family business succession done by Ivan Lansberg in his book, *Succeeding Generations*. It is required reading for families attempting long-term wealth preservation.

4. My complete thoughts on the role of elders in family governance may be found in Chapter 18. Here, I would like to recognize two very important considerations about elders. First, if the eldest generation of a family does not see an active, participatory role for itself in family governance, it is my experience that its fear of being rendered impotent in the life of its family will cause it to subvert the larger family's effort to create and sustain a family governance system. Second, if the wisdom of elders is

lost to a family, that loss represents not only the loss of its stories, its glue, but also the loss of the family's ability to do "seventh-generation thinking." Elders represent the wisdom of the Iroquois elder who says, as he begins the tribal council meeting, "Let us begin our work here today with the hope that the decisions we make will be honored by our tribal members seven generations from today." All family work, to be successful, must combine the freshness of the beginner's mind of youth with the ordered, evolutionary thinking of age. It is the conjunction of these two ways of thinking that offers the best path to successful family decision making. This is my father's wisdom, to "hasten slowly" when making difficult long-term choices extending out to the seventh generation.

5. It isn't the plan of this book to take the reader deeper into each of the other forms of governance that the framers of the Constitution might have chosen. It is my strong recommendation to every family I counsel that, early in their process of educating their members on their history and on their family's chosen system of governance, individual members undertake the same study of Aristotle's systems of governance as was made by the framers.

6. In Chapter 2, "The Family Mission Statement," I suggest a process that a family can use to discover and declare its values. Every family will discover though this process the things that make it unique.

PART TWO

Family Practices

Chapter Two

The Family
Mission Statement

E VERY WELL-MANAGED business in America has a mission statement. Accepting the metaphor that a family is a business, a
well-managed family should have a mission statement as well.

What is a mission statement? It is an expression of the purpose,
vision, values, and goals of a particular individual, couple, family, or
enterprise. The creation of a family mission statement is the starting
point for organizing the family to preserve its wealth. For a family
that is already organized, the need to express its purpose, values,
and goals will become apparent as soon as the first difficult problems arise and family members have no shared way of understanding how to resolve them. Wherever your family is in the process
of wealth preservation, a mission statement will help you achieve
long-term success. After all, if you can't define the mission of where
you're going, how will you know if you get there?

What are the issues a family mission statement needs to address
to define the family's purpose, vision, values, and goals?

• **A family needs to understand its purpose.** While I believe
the purpose of a family is to enhance the pursuit of happiness of its
individual members, and thereby preserve its human, intellectual,
and financial capital, each family must determine and define its philosophy for itself. The first goal of a mission statement is, therefore,
just that: to define the family's philosophy of its purpose.

- **A family must have a common vision.** It must look ahead to the future and form a consensus on a shared goal. A family should ask itself how it plans to achieve its current goals, while looking ahead twenty, fifty, and one hundred years, as discussed in Chapter 1. It must embrace the seventh-generation thinking of the Iroquois.
- **A family shares certain values.** I like to think that these are the values that create that family's uniqueness. In America this is a particularly difficult issue, because many Americans are uncomfortable thinking about themselves as "different." Americans still maintain the cultural myth of common membership in the middle class. Wealth automatically sets a family apart and makes it acutely sensitive to any suggestion that it is in fact different. How then to select the values that express a particular family's differentness? Later in this chapter, I've given some suggestions on how to do this.
- **A family needs to acknowledge its "secrets."** Every family believes that it knows secrets about itself and other families. In my experience of families and other forms of organization, and as John O'Neil teaches in his book *The Paradox of Success,* there are in fact no secrets. These apparent secrets are one of the most perfidious problems in family governance, and they sit invisibly on the liability side of a family's balance sheet. They can undermine a family faster than any other single liability.

Here is an example of the deleterious effect of unacknowledged secrets. I was once asked by a family to help it form a governing structure. The family prided itself on its close family ties, its successful annual meetings, and its general feeling of well-being. I wondered, with all these positives, what I could do to help. After interviewing the senior members of the family, I discovered that in fact the family's governance was in chaos because of secrets everyone thought they were keeping but everyone actually knew. One daughter was an alcoholic, a son was a drug addict, and another daughter was married to a man no one liked. When the family held meetings, none of these facts were acknowledged, so the problems went unaddressed. Their meetings consisted of platitudes about what a wonderful family they were and how well all members were doing. Not only was the family failing to preserve its financial wealth, it was draining its human and intellectual capital. It was in entropy. I pointed out to the senior members my views that these nonsecrets were undermining all of their wealth preservation efforts. Happily, they understood and ultimately agreed with me. The family is now on a changed course to real wealth preservation.

I'm sure some of you are concerned about confidentiality and about people being given financial information before they are educated to use it properly. Please understand that confidentiality in general and the dissemination of financial information to family members only as they are educated to absorb it are excellent values and ones to which I subscribe. These values can be stressed in a family mission statement. "Secrets," however, are pernicious, and a family mission statement should rule them out. I feel very strongly that the creation of a family mission statement provides the opportunity to discuss each family member's views on the subject of secrets, confidentiality, and the dissemination of information. The family mission statement should include a section reflecting the family's consensus on this subject and should recognize clearly the difference between the negative effects of protecting illusory secrets and the positive benefits of confidentiality.

• **A family needs to recount its history.** The preparation of a family mission statement affords a family an opportunity to tell its family stories. Family stories are the glue that binds together individual family members. Every family I know that is successfully preserving its wealth sets aside time at its family gatherings for the sharing of its unique history. Both young and old tell the stories and in this way discover their common bonds and values. A family mission statement should express the family's unique history.

• **A family must choose a form of governance.** Chapter 1 discusses the possible forms of governance. The family mission statement should indicate the form of governance selected by the family and how it will assist in long-term wealth preservation.

• **Each person needs to understand his or her role in the family.** A final purpose for the preparation of a family mission statement is the opportunity it affords each individual family member to consider her or his mission as a member of the family and as an individual. I recommend that each family member prepare a personal mission statement.

Here are the steps I recommend for preparing a family mission statement.

1) Agree to certain important rules for the conducting of family meetings. For these rules I am indebted to two of the important advisers in the field of counseling families, David Bork and Lee Hausner. David Bork sets out the Basque rules for holding a meeting, which I paraphrase as: Show up. Come to the meeting alert, ready to work, and having read any pre-meeting materials. Listen attentively. Don't interrupt the speaker, listen carefully, and be able to play back to the speaker what you heard to assure him or her you understood what was said.

Speak your truth without fear of blame or judgment. Understand that you are in a safe environment, where your views are solicited and respected.

Do not be committed to outcomes. The worst possible family meeting is one at which each member arrives with an expected outcome, creates an adversarial atmosphere, and goes home angry if he doesn't get the outcome he wanted. Family meetings are places to find consensus toward the long-term mission of wealth preservation. Any member's attachment to a short-term objective can create hurdles so high that they frustrate the achievement of long-term objectives. As in the Aristotelian republic, every member should come to the meeting with an open mind, then listen to the arguments, weigh them against his or her truth, and only then decide the disposition of that meeting's issues.

Lee Hausner, author of *Children of Paradise: Successful Parenting for Prosperous Families,* adds a special rule for all family meetings: "Never start a sentence with the word 'But' when replying to something a family member said." Lee argues that if you start a sentence with the word "But," you are telling the other speaker you didn't listen affirmatively to what was said. The word "but" suggests that you are going to refute something, not discuss it. This rule, while difficult to learn, has in my experience significantly helped achieve consensus while, happily, shortening meetings.

A final rule for family meetings is that a chairperson and secretary must be selected for that particular meeting. The chair's role is to facilitate the meeting as one among equals, not to act as if she or he were the traditional chairman of the board. Remember, it's first participation and then consensus the family is seeking to help it in its effort to achieve its mission. The secretary's role is to take the minutes of the meeting and to evaluate and collect comments on the draft minutes following the meeting. I cannot stress strongly enough the need for minutes. Great damage has occurred in many families because a clear record of decisions did not exist. These minutes also serve to preserve the family history and are a critical resource for later generations. Many family advisers suggest rotating these tasks to give all members a chance to learn these important functions. I agree, with the caveat that these roles should be agreed on after the meeting agenda is set so that individuals who will have major reports to make at that meeting are not also charged with one of these responsibilities.

2) For a family's first meeting on governance, each family member should prepare a personal résumé. You probably believe you know just about everything significant about your family members. Let me surprise you by advising you that you're wrong. In my experience family members know very little about each other, and what they do know is seriously dated. Our basic view of other family members is vertical, assaying where he or she fits on the family tree. In my experience, we rarely know more than the general circumstances of anyone in our extended family. Often we aren't even up-to-date on what our siblings or nieces and nephews are doing. The preparation of personal résumés gives each family member a chance to look at who she or he is and then to share that view with the other family members. These résumés should include everything the particular family member believes her or his best friend might know. These résumés, to be truly useful, must go far beyond the schools we attended and jobs we do; they must include the expression of our passions. After all, our passions express our individual pursuits of happiness.

Before family members prepare these résumés I remind them

that each is a crucial human asset on the family's balance sheet. I explain that preparation of these résumés will permit the compilation of a human resources inventory so the family will know what its human capital is, and so that the representatives of the family know where in the family to find the expertise they need. Human resources inventories help families to effectively use their human assets in carrying out projects. Too frequently families fail to engage their human assets, which can lead to hurt feelings and to the loss of opportunity to build human and intellectual capital.

I suggest the preparation of résumés take fifteen minutes.

Once the personal résumés are completed and shared, I suggest that each family member, after the meeting, prepare a personal mission statement as a further guide to personal learning. While this is not a required step, it is much easier to prepare a family mission statement when each member is aware of her or his individual mission.

3) Each family member should write the ten values he or she considers most crucial to the family's long-term success. These values are posted on the wall as each member offers his or her list. Through this process the entire family value system is captured and synthesized. Ultimately, the values that reflect family consensus are compiled into a family mission statement. Where the family membership exceeds twenty people, smaller groups compile lists of values and report back to the larger assembly.

Allot twenty minutes of meeting time for family members to present their values.

4) Each family member should write what each would, at the age of 105, tell her or his immediate family had been most important to her or him in life. Within a small group these can be shared orally, and in a larger group archived as a part of the human resources inventory. This exercise elicits long-term thinking about critical family issues and when synthesized offers long-term objectives helpful in the process of creating the family mission statement.

Allot twenty minutes of meeting time for the sharing of these long-term values.

5) Each family member should write a description of the family twenty years hence. This exercise helps family members begin to understand the long-term nature of the process they are undertaking. Allot thirty minutes for presentation of these descriptions.

6) A small committee should write a brief family history. Place a special emphasis on past family crises and opportunities, on the personalities of famous and infamous ancestors whose impact is still felt, and on past successes and failures in making family decisions. Allot one hour for review of the family history.

7) Finally, the family should create its own government. In Chapter 1, I discuss the different forms of government history offers to us, and I explain why I believe Aristotle is right that a republic is the best form of governance for human beings. In its first meeting, the family should describe the forms of governance set out by Aristotle in *The Politics* and then break into groups to discuss which system of governance will best achieve the family's long-term goal of wealth preservation. This gives each member of the family an experience in making government and an understanding of what the members of the Constitutional Convention accomplished in writing the Constitution of the United States. Creating a family mission statement is, above all, an act of governance.

Once these exercises are completed, the family has all of the resources and skills necessary to prepare a family mission statement. By going through these steps, the family will also have gained a profound sense of the aspirations of each family member and experienced the thrill of working together to achieve a common purpose.

This process creates a template for holding successful family meetings and a model for the family to use to find consensus on much more difficult problems. Here are a few more pieces of advice that will help your family create a solid initial mission statement.

First—Be bold. All too often families don't know how strong they are and how much they can accomplish.

Second—Understand the power of teams. Families after all are groups of two or more. In business schools, the teaching paradigm has long been teams, not individuals. Families who are successful at preserving their wealth know this paradigm and use it.

Third—Remember, this is just the first draft. Don't worry if your mission statement isn't perfect. Do the best you can, but don't overdo.

Fourth—Have fun. Nothing beats humor in building human bonds.

Chapter Three

Ritual

FAMILIES WHO RECOGNIZE with ritual the important passages in their members' lives seem to fare better at overcoming the shirtsleeves proverb. This should not be surprising, since the creation and practice of rituals marking important developmental steps in the life of a human being are at the core of successful tribal life.

Tribes are the extended generations of an original family. Anthropology teaches that a tribe is the result of a family in its second or third generation having formed clans, and then of those clans in the fourth and fifth generations electing to stay together, thus eventually creating a tribe. From such beginnings many tribes have successfully continued for dozens of generations, thus overcoming the shirtsleeves proverb. The Iroquois are a good example.

Clearly, a tribe is not based solely on genetic ties, given the small amount of unique DNA it shares from a common ancestor. Rather, it is the stories of the experiences and practices of the early generations that link these people as a tribe. These linkages are part of what defines a tribe as a family of affinity rather than merely of blood. The rituals that tribes create, often unique to them and representing their "differentness," arise from their stories and experiences. These rituals offer the tribe's members a way of linking themselves to their ancestors, to their stories, to the uniqueness of their tribe, and to their special place in it.

What is the nature of ritual and its place in the development of an individual, and of the family or tribe of which he or she is a part?

In his book *Rites of Passage,* Arnold Van Gennep explains how a family's or tribe's rituals assist the individual's successful development at various stages of life. Such rituals allow the individual to break away from an earlier developmental stage; learn the new information needed for the next stage; and be reintegrated into the tribe, ready to begin the next stage of development and contribute to the successful life of the tribe.

Ritual thus serves two purposes in the life of a family seeking to thrive for many generations. It helps individuals develop from one life stage to another, and it helps the family succeed by promoting the development of its members. The whole family is strengthened in its process of development from family to clan to tribe, for many generations into the future.

What are some of the important life stages of family members, and of the family as a whole, that rituals might be created to honor?

First: Coming of age. All tribes and many religious communities recognize the transition from childhood to adulthood with ritual. Often such rituals involve the younger members' being taken away from their parents and being taught the tribe's or religious community's secrets, its mysteries. In many earlier societies the teaching role was assigned to the child's aunts, uncles, or tribal elders.[1] In religious communities this role was given to the priests and priestesses. Such ritual processes often involved the child living apart from the tribe with other children the same age. This is Van Gennep's breaking-away stage. While living apart, the young person received knowledge about the tribe's or religious community's special wisdom and discovered his or her own special talents and how they could be used to help the tribe as a whole—Van Gennep's second stage. Finally, the newly fledged adult member was reintegrated into tribal life (Van Gennep's third stage), often gaining a new name. Elaborate rituals were developed to recognize this successful reintegration of tribal members.

Second: A new elder. All successful families and tribes recognize the need for elders for good governance. My view of the importance of elders in family governance was, I hope, made clear in Chapter 1. The creation of a new elder is an extremely important point in the development of a family or tribe, because it reflects the willingness of the group to grant to an individual the authority to mediate its disputes, point out when it isn't following the rules of governance, and maintain its stories. The evolution of a family member to this status is also a major developmental step, because it shows that this member has finished doing his or her individual work and is now seen as wise and ready to act for the family as a whole. Many tribes mark this granting of authority with rituals.

Third: The arrival of a new member. Rituals acknowledging the birth of a new family or tribe member, or the marrying-in of a new member, are very important. All tribes and religious communities recognize with elaborate celebrations the birth of new members. These rituals not only announce the individual's arrival but also offer the tribe or religious community a way of reaffirming the many prior generations from which this child springs. More important, a ritual offers members of the tribe a means to celebrate and reaffirm the possibilities for their future. Ritual is also important in this case to give the family, tribe, or religious community a way of committing itself to the legitimacy of this child and thus of his or her right to nurturance and future membership.

The marrying-in of a new member is another important developmental step in the life both of the individual entering the family and of the family itself. All families, tribes, and religious communities elaborately recognize a marriage. The rituals surrounding the entry of a new member celebrate the growth of the community and legitimize the new member's right to be a part of that community. Such rituals recognize that this new member is breaking away from another tribe and needs information about the mysteries of the tribe he or she is joining, and such rituals offer a process by which the new member can be integrated into a new set of relationships.

Fourth: The death of a member. Most families, tribes, and religious communities observe the death of a member with ritual.

Such rites honor the life of the deceased member, assist surviving members with grieving, and provide a way to integrate the deceased member's life into the stories that link him or her to the ongoing life of the family, the tribe, or the religious community.

Fifth: The introduction of new outside members. Families seeking to govern themselves well introduce into their midst trustees, protectors, mentors, advisers, and *hommes d'affaires*. In later chapters I elaborate on the important, even critical, roles in family governance that such outsiders play. Rituals to celebrate the arrival of such individuals into the lives of family members, and of the family as a whole, are an important celebration of their role and a legitimization of their future authority and responsibility in family life and governance. A ritual for their welcoming announces and establishes their proper position in family life. It makes it much more likely that, having been welcomed by the family as a whole and through ritual properly indoctrinated into the families' life and governance, they will successfully perform their roles and functions.

What are some of the forms of ritual a family can study in developing its own unique rituals?

Most religious communities have rituals such as baptism, naming, confirmation, bar or bat mitzvah, marriage, ordination, last rights, and funerals to recognize the developmental stages of their members. Many of these rituals can be modified by a family to celebrate the developmental stages of its members. Secular communities, whether monarchies, dictatorships, or republics, use music, speeches, special dress, dance, food and beverage, elections, graduations, marriages, and funerals to celebrate the developmental stages of their members and of their communities. Many of these forms of ritual can and are modified by families to celebrate their birthdays, marriages, anniversaries, and deaths. Cultural anthropology also offers many examples of the unique ways in which human communities have evolved rites to celebrate the stages of development of individual members of tribes.

The range and creativity of rituals celebrating developmental stages is astonishingly broad. Clearly such rituals are integral to successful individual and family growth. Apparently all human beings sense the need for such celebrations as a way of affirming the critical steps in the development of each individual and for the survival of the families and tribes of which they are a part. We all seem to sense that there are moments when we must break away from one stage of life, learn new things, and then reintegrate as more developed beings into the families and communities of which we are a part. Ritual strengthens our bonds to our families and increases the likelihood of our and their long-term survival and success.

May each of your families celebrate these important moments of change as critical steps in your families' developments, through the unique rituals that you design. As you do so you will discover your "differentness," add to the family stories, and most importantly, honor and grow your family's human and intellectual capital. In all these ways you will add to your family's wealth.

Chapter Notes

1. For a specific discussion of the critical roles of aunts and uncles in the use of ritual in developing younger members of families, see Chapter 16.

Chapter Four

The Family Balance Sheet and Family Income Statement

T HE FAMILY BALANCE sheet and family income statement are key tools for measuring the health of a family's long-term wealth preservation business. As with any business, the shareholders—in this case, family members—need to know how the enterprise is doing, so they need a way of measuring the business's progress. These measurements allow shareholders to instruct the directors, managers, and trustees of the family business on the tasks of running it and to determine how well these managers are fulfilling their roles.

The traditional balance sheet attempts to measure the state of well-being of a business at a certain point in time. Such balance sheets contain statements of assets, liabilities, and shareholder equity as a reflection of the business's financial status. The family balance sheet also lists assets, liabilities, and shareholder equity but expands what each category measures. Because successful long-term family wealth preservation is achieved by enhancing the well-being of individual family members over a long period of time, the family balance sheet measures human and intellectual capital as well as financial capital. The family balance sheet is an attempt to measure how well a family is managing its human capital.

A family balance sheet is an addition to, not a substitute for, a family financial statement. A family wealth management busi-

THE FAMILY BALANCE SHEET*

ASSETS   MINUS →   LIABILITIES

The family's total human capital, including:

- Each family member's intellectual capital
- Each family member's financial capital
- Each family member's social capital

Long-term family risks

- Failure of family governance
- Failure to understand that success requires a one-hundred-year plan
- Failure to comprehend and manage all forms of family capital, human and intellectual as well as financial

Intermediate family risks (internal)

- Death   • Divorce
- Addiction and other "secrets"
- Malthus's Law (the geometric increase of family members in each generation)
- Creditors   • Poor health
- Poor beneficiary/trustee relationships
- Investment programs of less than fifty years

Intermediate family risks (external)

- Inflation
- Inadequate trustee management
- Estate and other forms of transfer and wealth taxes
- Holocaust
- Acts of God
- Changes of political system
- Lack of personal security

Short-term family risks

- Income taxes   • Market fluctuation
- No mission statement
- Lack of financial education

EQUALS →   SHAREHOLDER EQUITY

- Are individual family members successfully pursuing happiness?
- Are the family's human capital and intellectual capital increasing when measured against the family's liabilities?
- Is the family as a whole dynamically preserving itself?
- Is the family's governance system producing more good decisions than bad by taking a seventh-generational view?

Special thanks to Charlotte Beyer and The Institute for Private Investors for their invaluable assistance in the creation of this work.

ness, like every other financial organization, must know its financial capacity to carry on its mission.

The Family Balance Sheet

Business balance sheets reflect a point in time, but when combined with previous balance sheets, they can reveal short- and long-term trends. Most company balance sheets report results backward and forward over specific time periods in order to measure trends and to show the business's progress. Business defines two years as short-term, five years as intermediate, and ten years as long-term. Families assess their wealth preservation with an analogous system and for the same purposes but use different time periods. Unfortunately, very few families have understood how long-term their measurement has to be to know if they are successful. They look at time periods that are much too short—five years, or ten, perhaps. But families attempting to overcome the "Shirtsleeves to shirtsleeves in three generations" proverb should define short-term as twenty years, or one generation; intermediate as fifty years, or two generations; and long-term as one hundred years, or three generations. This difference of view profoundly affects the nature of the assets and liabilities being measured. It also enforces very long-term planning. A family balance sheet should report to its shareholders the historic results of the family's long-term wealth preservation business using these longer time periods.

INVESTMENT TIME HORIZONS

	IN AN ORDINARY BUSINESS	IN THE FAMILY BUSINESS OF LONG-TERM WEALTH PRESERVATION
Short term	2 years	20 years (one generation)
Intermediate term	5 years	50 years (two generations)
Long term	10 years	100 years (three generations)

When families create a family balance sheet in this form, they quickly appreciate the actual position of the family vis-à-vis the shirtsleeves proverb. Applying the state of the family as reflected on the family balance sheet to the mission of the family as stated in its family mission statement, the family can begin to do the required long-term strategic planning. With this tool each family member can learn to act as a shareholder of the family business and understand his or her role in it.

The Income Statement

Ordinary businesses use annual income statements to reflect profits and losses over a single year. Family businesses need to compile analogous documents, called family income statements. When used with the family balance sheet, the family income statement measures the increase or decrease in the family's human and intellectual capital during the year in question, and thus measures the family's annual performance in managing its human and intellectual capital. Family leaders collect and review family members' résumés and individual mission statements, as described in Chapter 2, to assess gains and losses in human and intellectual capital. I recommend to families as a "best practice" for successful family governance that they obtain an updated résumé and personal mission statement from each member annually. This practice gives the family governance leaders a clear impression of how the individual family members who form the assets on the family balance sheet are doing in their individual pursuits of happiness. It will also tell them whether the family as a whole has increased or decreased its human and intellectual capital during the year being measured.

When a family holds financial assets in trust, the family income statement should also include a summary by the family's governance leaders of two other sets of reports:

- annual reports by family members of themselves as beneficiaries, based on beneficiary best practices (see Chapter 10); and
- annual reports by family trustees on their performance in light of trustee best practices (see Chapter 11).

The results of these reviews alert the family leaders to current and future liabilities on the family balance sheet. They offer the leaders an opportunity to address these issues as they emerge so they can be managed before they turn into serious problems.

Families who create a family balance sheet and family income statement are amazed at how rich they are in human and intellectual capital. They are even more amazed at how much better they do financially within two to three years of implementing these practices. Why are their results so rewarding? If the family leaders know what their human and intellectual capital is, they can engage each family member as a shareholder in the mission of the family business: long-term wealth preservation. Once family members are engaged in this process, the overall risk profile of the family declines.

Chapter Five

Investor Allocation

This chapter is dedicated to Charlotte Beyer, founder of the Institute for Private Investors, who is successfully educating families on their roles as investors.

INVESTOR ALLOCATION IS a powerful tool on the revenue side of a family's financial balance sheet. This chapter assumes that the older generation is anxious to increase the financial wealth of the younger generation—a goal not universally held by American families. Many of America's greatest modern wealth creators, men like Warren Buffett and Bill Gates, have said publicly that they intend to leave the bulk of their fortunes to philanthropy while leaving only modest sums to their children. These wealth creators believe that unearned wealth risks corrupting the individuals receiving it by depriving them of the dignity of work and by interfering with the creative life choices later generations of the family would make if they were not burdened by wealth they did not create. These wealth creators believe long-term family wealth preservation lies in each generation's being the first generation of wealth creators, within the individual capabilities of each member to create his or her own wealth.

This is the same idea I discussed in Chapter 1 as a foundation principle for successful long-term wealth preservation. However, I do not fully agree with the views and methodologies of these wealth creators. I represent children and grandchildren of wealth creators who practice this philosophy, and often these children and grand-children are just as financially and psychologically dependent on the wealth creator as in families practicing the opposite philosophy.

Neither the receipt nor the deprivation of financial capital leads to a successful life. It is only through the older generation's active enhancement of the younger generation's individual pursuits of happiness that a new generation of wealth creators can be born.

Investor allocation in this context is the allocation to each family member on the family balance sheet (whether the member is an individual or a trust, a pooled vehicle, or a philanthropy) of that portion of the family's financial assets most likely to assist the long-term growth of those financial assets while minimizing U.S., estate, gift, or generation-skipping transfer taxation.[1]

Most of us are familiar with modern portfolio theory and its admonition that 90 percent of successful long-term investing lies in correct asset allocation. As I am not an investment professional, I will not comment further on this theory. I will, however, assume that if you are not familiar with the theory of asset allocation, your investment adviser can offer an expert explanation. I also recommend Charles D. Ellis's book *Winning the Loser's Game—Timeless Strategies for Successful Investing* (McGraw-Hill Trade, 2002) as an excellent study of investing.

Families who are successful investors have elaborate asset allocation plans. Their investment portfolios often include equities, bonds, real estate, collectibles, venture capital, oil and gas, and alternative investments, including hedge funds. All too often, however, the individual family members holding these investments were not chosen on the basis of how far they are removed from estate or gift taxation but rather by "who had cash" when the investment opportunity arose. Unfortunately for long-term tax avoidance, it is often the oldest member of a family who is wealthiest or "has the cash" when the investment opportunity arises, so it is she or he who buys it. The result over time is that the oldest family members hold many of the fastest-growing assets on the family financial balance sheet. In fact, these older members are often encouraged by their investment advisers to grow their portfolios to assure more funds for later generations. At the same time, the older members of a family are often the most risk averse and would prefer to hold assets producing more income.

An investment program in which the oldest member of the family acquires growth securities brings a huge smile to the face of the Internal Revenue Service. The IRS knows that if it waits patiently, it will collect more than half of the stock's growth as estate tax. Why? Because, assuming Grandmother's estate exceeds $4 million, which puts her estate in the highest estate tax bracket of 55 percent, the IRS will get $0.55 of each $1 of growth. The IRS, believe it or not, is sitting in the largest chair at the family table.[2]

Investor allocation can reduce the size of the IRS's chair year after year until it is the smallest at the family table. How? By reinvesting each new dollar of family wealth in the following way. Each time the family's investment adviser suggests a new investment, the family member, family office professional, or other adviser charged with investor allocation determines the investment's projected long-term growth rate. The "investor allocator" then chooses the family member or members who will actually make the investment based on estate tax implications. Normally, this means the oldest family member buys the investments offering the lowest growth, and the youngest family member buys the investments offering the highest growth.

Two investment classes can act as examples. Suppose the family wants to invest $100 in bonds that will be held to maturity and on which the family will receive current interest payments. This investment offers no growth of principal—the investor expects to receive, upon maturity, the same amount originally invested. Now let us suppose the family wants to invest $100 in venture capital. Let's assume the goal is to double the value of the investment over five years. In that event the family will receive $200 for the $100 it invested, growing its principal by $100. Clearly the IRS would be delighted if Grandmother bought the venture capital investment, since the IRS will get $55 of that $100 profit upon her death. The IRS would be commensurately unhappy if Grandmother bought the bonds and a younger family member bought the venture capital investment. The IRS would be particularly unhappy if Grandmother bought the bonds and used them as collateral for borrowing by a grandchild who, without the loan, couldn't afford to make the venture capital investment. Grandmother is doubly happy since she will receive current income from the bonds, whereas she wouldn't ordinarily receive any return on the venture capital investment for five years. The family is delighted because Grandmother's estate didn't grow even though the family financial balance sheet grew by $100.

This example of investor allocation, while quite simple, makes the point. Obviously, there are many other types of investments, carrying varying degrees of risk, between the two categories I chose for the example. Every asset allocation program, properly made, will have investment classes throughout the risk universe. The point of investor allocation is to manage this risk universe by maximizing growth of the overall family financial balance sheet while minimizing the growth of the individual portfolios most likely to be the next to be subject to estate tax.

Families with whom I work who employ this strategy are excited by how quickly they see results from it. Happily, the IRS has no authority to decide which investments each member of a family makes.

To obtain maximum benefit from investor allocation, here are some issues a family will need to address.

• The family's mission statement should include a commitment to long-term wealth preservation. Successful investor allocation requires that each family member elect to participate in investor allocation after careful consideration of his or her individual investment goals, as well as his or her commitment to the family's wealth preservation strategy.

• Family members, directors of family philanthropies, managers of family investment vehicles, and trustees of family trusts should all agree to participate in the investor allocation program in the same positive spirit with which they participate in the family's overall asset allocation process.

• Families need bold trustees to implement an investor allocation program. Trustees have special legal responsibilities that govern their behavior as investors. Under these responsibilities, a trustee cannot give up ultimate discretion over the investment policy of the trust he oversees. The investor allocator will need to be mindful of those trustee responsibilities. Hopefully, the family trust instruments will grant the trustees the broadest possible investment discretion. Such a broad grant of investment authority will make it simpler for the trustees to accept their investment allocations within the family's overall asset allocation plan. The trustees' need for broad investment discretion is particularly necessary if higher-risk investments are to be allocated to the trusts.

• In constructing an investor allocation program, the youngest members of a family and the family's longest-term estate tax and generation-skipping-transfer-tax-free trusts should acquire the assets with the greatest growth potential. The portfolios of these family members and trusts should match the family's long-term or one-hundred-year investment horizon. The oldest family members should acquire the lowest-growth assets, to meet the family's twenty-year horizon, and intermediate generations should take positions in accordance with the family's fifty-year horizon. You will quickly apprehend that the plan works best when the youngest family members and the long-term family trusts that are exempt from estate taxation and generation-skipping transfer taxation have the most money, and the oldest members of the family the least. Obviously this is not the normal situation; it is highly unusual. The problem, therefore, is how to get assets to the youngest family members and to the exempt long-term trusts so that they can make the desired long-term investments.

One way to solve the problem is by gifts. Unfortunately, U.S. gift tax law places low limits on how much can be given before taxes begin to accrue. The most successful strategy is for the oldest generation to make loans to the youngest generation—and in certain cases, after ·careful legal advice, to the tax-exempt long-term trusts—to enable acquisition of the appropriate assets. Intrafamily loans carry with them certain IRS responsibilities to ensure that they are arm's-length loans and not disguised gifts. A lending strategy should not be developed without proper legal and accounting advice to ensure that loans are not recharacterized as gifts. An important additional benefit of this strategy is the receipt of high cash flows by the oldest generation through their receipt of interest on their loans while the growth of a portion of their assets is capped. The additional cash flow will meet their desire for cash and also provide them with additional liquidity to make gifts to family and philanthropy and to make additional loans. As with any investment decision, careful analysis of the role of such loans in the family's and the individual lenders' overall investment programs must be made to determine what portion of an individual's portfolio might be devoted to this program. (This same strategy, but with a larger purpose, is discussed in Chapter 7, "The Family Bank.")

If a lending plan is adopted, careful thought must be given to the problem of repayment. Again, legal and accounting advice should be taken to assure that necessary collateral and liquidity issues are carefully planned for.

Investor allocation supports long-term family wealth preservation. It employs the family's financial and intellectual capital toward successful wealth preservation while managing down the estate tax and generation-skipping transfer tax liability on the family balance sheet.

Chapter Notes

1. This book assumes the reader has a general understanding of these forms of taxation. Proper consultation with excellent tax advisers should be taken, however, before using the financial tools discussed in this chapter.

2. Some states also have forms of taxation at death that can result in combined state and federal rates as high as 63 percent. Readers should discuss with their financial advisers the estate tax position in their state.

Chapter Six

Two Important Practices

I N MY DAY-TO-DAY work with families, two practices have emerged as especially helpful. Each practice deals with skills family members can learn that will improve their ability to manage the multiple relationships they share. I use both of these practices as fundamental building blocks in teaching families how to practice good family governance.

Hat Work

The first is founded on the work of Ernest Doud and Lee Hausner in their book *Hats Off to You*. In their book, Ernie and Lee recount the story of a father and son who are in business together. The father was the founder of the company, and the son worked there. The father's calling had been to found and own this very successful enterprise. The son, although he had a very high opinion of himself and his work for the company, didn't share his father's calling and was generally seen as incompetent by his coworkers. One day, an opportunity arose in the company's senior ranks, and the son assumed that he would be promoted to this position. His father invited him home for lunch, and the son assumed the purpose of the lunch was to announce and celebrate his promotion. The son arrived and found his father at poolside. On the luncheon table were two hats. On one was written "Boss" and on the other "Dad." His father welcomed him, asked him to sit down, and put on the hat labeled "Boss." The father then said, "Son, you are fired." The father immediately took off the first hat and put on the one labeled "Dad." He put his arm around his son's shoulders and said, "Son, your mother and I are deeply concerned that you are unemployed. How can we help you?" With this story, Doud and Hausner are informing families that within every family relationship are embedded multiple other relationships.

In my work with three-generation families with financial capital, I often find that when I diagram the relationships of any two members of the family to each other, and then to all the others, they have as many as twenty-one relationships. For example, a family member may simultaneously be a grandchild, child, sibling, niece, cousin, spouse, aunt or uncle, and parent, as well as a beneficiary, trustee, board member, employee, stockholder, or partner in various family enterprises.

My colleague Joanie Bronfman and I are constantly increasing the number of relationships of these types that we discover in the families we work with, as the ingenuity of the families' advisers bring new forms of enterprise into these families' structures.

One of the things that we recommend families do at their governance meetings is to make a diagram of the family as a whole, of all of their interwoven relationships, and then make a similar diagram of all the individual relationships each family member shares with all of the other family members. This practice informs the family of what it actually looks like as a living beehive or ant farm and informs each individual of how he or she relates to every other family member and to the family as a whole. For family members and their advisers to understand the complexity of a family's relationships and their unique character as a composite of those relationships helps the family to understand how it exists and how it functions.

In addition to understanding current relationships I recommend that families look into their pasts to find the teachers of the spirit, the discoverers, and the creators who in earlier generations forged the ideas and practices that underlie the family's current ways of being and dealing with each other. I suggest that they diagram their relations and connections to earlier generations and particularly to those three categories of ancestors. By making such diagrams, families can see themselves through the lenses of their history, better understand how their "differentness" evolved, and understand why they act as they do.[1]

Once a family has made such diagrams, its members can then begin to take apart each past and current relationship and study it. They can begin to learn what practices and skills that relationship requires to achieve competence in its management. Again, thanks to Doud and Hausner's book, we have an exceptional method for learning how to practice each relationship once we set out the list of skills needed for its success. Doud and Hausner suggest employing hats of different colors to represent the parties to the relationship being learned. In my practice, after a family has diagrammed its relationships, we often practice the beneficiary/ trustee relationship first. I begin with this relationship because it is often one all family members share; because it is less personal in that it often includes a nonfamily member; because it is frequently a thoroughly misunderstood relationship, as later chapters of this book will discuss; and finally because if the relationship fails it can lead quickly and in my experience irretrievably to a failure of the whole family structure.

How does a family execute this practice? I suggest that a red hat and a blue hat be purchased for every family member before the meeting in which the family will do this exercise. I then ask each family member to put on a red hat and assume the role of beneficiary of a trust. We then develop together the skill set, the roles and responsibilities, that a beneficiary needs to practice to become a "great" beneficiary. Everyone then takes off the red hat and puts on the blue one, thereby assuming the role of trustee. We then develop together the roles and responsibilities of a trustee. Finally we pair off and act out the different roles and responsibilities that underlie the beneficiary/trustee relationship, each of the pair wearing the hat representing the role he or she is assuming in the relationship. Expressing each of the parts of the relationship while wearing the color representing that role is astonishingly powerful in helping each family member feel and experience the roles and responsibilities the two parts of this relationship represent.

My mentor and friend Dan Garvey has taught me that for any learning to be useful, it must be experienced and integrated into the student's life and become a part of his or her intellectual capital. The hats exercise—"What hat am I wearing?"—is the best tool I know to allow family members to experience each of their multiple relationships and to enable that family member to integrate that experience. I strongly recommend to families that at each family meeting they facilitate this process of learning together about the multiple relationships they share by taking apart one such relationship and using the hats exercise to understand how that relationship works, what skills are needed to practice it at its best, and hopefully thereby to achieve excellence in its practice.

It is my experience that the largest number of problems families experience in their governance flow from their lack of understanding of the skills needed for each of their many relationships. As we all know, if we cannot establish the boundaries of a relationship, we are likely to be unable to live successfully within it. Most of us, however, have only one or two relationships where we need to learn special skills in order to practice them well and enjoy the benefits that can grow out of them. Families often don't recognize the multiplicity of their relationships and founder on that failure as they fail to manage their many relationships successfully. Families in my experience often don't recognize where one relationship within their system abuts another, and they fail thereby to establish the boundaries necessary for each relationship to be successful. If, however, a family can be helped to see how complicated this process is when its members may be in as many as twenty-one separate relationships with the same people, each of which is being acted out at the same time, and with the multiple boundary issues each of these relationships represents, then there is hope for that family's ability to successfully self govern. The practice of "What hat am I wearing?" offers a family a powerful tool for studying and practicing each of those intertwined relationships.

As I write this second edition of this book I am beginning with a few families to expand this exercise by adding a third party, who at different times wears a white or a black hat. Many years ago Murray Bowen, among his many extraordinary insights into the workings of families, informed us of the problem of triangling.[2] This is the problem of family relationships in which three parties are involved and which often form the basis for great family dysfunction and individual unhappiness. While I am not qualified from a professional viewpoint to discuss this issue further with families, and thankfully there are many skilled practitioners who are (hats off to them!), I do feel comfortable in pointing out to families the power of triangles, for good and for bad.

The triangle is the strongest geometric form in the universe and so should be empowering when found and used. In my work with families on their multiple relationships, a third party wearing a white hat represents the outside party who strengthens the relationship between the parties wearing red and blue hats. In the case of the beneficiary/trustee relationship, this party might be the protector discussed in Chapter 8. A third party wearing a black hat represents ignorance of how the relationship is meant to work, a third person in the triangle who twists it out of shape and weakens it irrevocably. The person wearing the black hat might take the role of a litigious attorney, a fortune-hunting spouse, or an ignorant friend just wanting to help out. Asking a family to add these two colors to the "What hat am I wearing?" exercise deepens their experience of the relationship they are acting out. Further, using three colors assists them in understanding the truth of Bowen's observations for the strengthening and weakening of family relationships described by triangling.

I offer this addition to the hats exercise while asking you to appreciate that my experience in using it is short. I would not suggest it, however, if I did not believe it would be generally helpful. The risk I see in using it is that it may bring up difficult unresolved issues of existing weak triangles within the family's relationships. I strongly recommend, therefore, that if a family decides to add the white and black hats to the "What hat am I wearing?" exercise it do so only, as I do, with a trained Bowenian facilitator who is competent to deal with unexpected relationship issues that may emerge from what otherwise may seem a "safe" exercise. My goal is to help families, and to not do harm. Please heed my admonition!

Grandchild/Grandparent Philanthropy

The second practice I have found useful can be introduced by reinterpreting a Chinese proverb, "Grandparents and grandchildren are the natural enemies of the parents," as "Grandparents and grandchildren are natural allies." History and literature, as well as my own personal experience, all indicate that a grandparent's relationship with his or her grandchildren is filled with pure love. Grandparenting offers the chance to teach the family positive virtues, stories, and myths without the parental obligation of being concerned with discipline and passing on by admonition the family's negative experiences.

Often in my work with families, the grandparents ask me what role they can play in family governance. Frequently they feel unsure of their direct relationships with their adult children and are all too aware of the missteps that they made in parenting. They seek with their children a mature modus vivendi, while recognizing that past difficulties in their relationship cannot be expunged. Necessarily with this history, the roles in family governance of older parents and their adult children are those of equals seeking to preserve the family. Also, given their respective ages, the children will normally be taking on the active governance responsibilities in investing and administering the family wealth. The senior generation will be moving to the roles of observers and, most importantly, to acting as elders when a need for dispute resolution arises. While the latter role is critical to successful family governance, it is by its nature rarely called upon. Given the longevity of individuals today, limiting sixty-five-year-olds to basically passive roles in family governance simply wastes the vitality of significant family assets. At the same time, not to permit the rising generation to assume the active roles in family governance will lead to its frustration, and a different waste of family assets will occur.

Recognizing the desirability of using all family assets fully, I believe that within the special relationship between grandparents and grandchildren, families can better employ the vitality and wisdom of their elders. I suggest that families employ philanthropy as the means to accomplishing this end. Philanthropy, in and of itself, is a practical teaching tool for learning virtues through the process of giving to others. Philanthropy, as a vehicle for grandparents to take an active role in family governance, offers a means for them to teach their grandchildren the family's values and particularly the values of gratitude and stewardship. This gives grandchildren and grandparents a particularly powerful role in family governance.[3]

How would such a philanthropy work? First, I recommend that families start small, because even gifts of $50 or $100 will seem very large to young children.

Second, I suggest using the simplest structure possible. If the family already has a significant private philanthropy, I suggest it set aside a small portion of the capital for this specific purpose. If such a philanthropy does not exist, a "donor advised fund" can be arranged with most community foundations for amounts of $10,000 or more.

Third, I suggest that the philanthropy include all the grandchildren age six and over. In some of the families I serve, there is an age spread among the grandchildren of more than twenty years. Despite this age difference, I find that the commonality of the grandchildren's love and admiration for their grandparents creates a bond that overcomes the age gap. In addition, in families that have trusts, frequently the grandchildren form a class of beneficiaries that makes no distinction regarding age. As a class, all the grandchildren share the same financial interests in the trust. This similarity of financial position frequently leads to a need for the older grandchildren to mentor and lead the younger ones in their common situations. This similarity of situations forms another bridge of commonality within the group.

Fourth, grandchildren age twelve and older should form an investment and administrative committee for the philanthropy. While we can easily see the benefits that come from philanthropy in learning to give, we often fail to appreciate that a philanthropy is a business and can provide an educational setting for acquiring needed investment and administrative skills that are immediately transferable to the for-profit section of a family's activities. I strongly urge that the grandparents give the investment and administrative responsibilities to the older grandchildren as soon as possible. The grandparents should act as mentors and advisers, retaining, of course, ultimate decision making until they are confident of their grandchildren's capabilities.

Fifth, I suggest that all the grandchildren and the grandparents form the grants committee. I believe it is important that each grandchild make a grant each year. The process of how the grant is requested and voted on is critical to the learning experience of the grandchild and to the grandparents' ability to mentor the process. I believe that any child age six or older is capable of proposing and advocating a grant request. Obviously the older the grandchild, the more written material regarding the grant recipient should be required. When grandchildren are age ten or older, I also strongly suggest that, as a part of their requests, they make site visits to the proposed grantee or, if this is impossible, interview its director.

Although the written material and site visits are important, the truly important part of the grant request process is the oral presentation by the requesting grandchild at the annual meeting of the grandchild/grandparent philanthropy. At this meeting, each grant advocate should be called on to present her or his grant proposal. Following the presentation, the grandparents and the other grandchildren should, with great care and affection, critique the request and then vote on the application. The questions, suggestions, and possible additional homework required to assure that the grant will be used wisely should be tailored to the grandchild's age. For young-adult grandchildren, the grandparents may require that they also "put their skin in the game" by actively participating in the organization to which their requested grant will be made and by adding funds of their own to the philanthropy's grant.

From the grandparents' perspective, what could be more fun than to sit with one's grandchildren, discuss their passions, and discover who they are? From the grandchildren's perspective, what could be more beneficial than to get to know their grandparents through their wisdom and the stories of their own giving, to deepen their knowledge and respect for them, and, with great fun, to be taught the family's wisdom and rituals?

Sixth, it is very important that the parents of the grandchildren be excluded as much as possible from this process. The exclusion is not an unfriendly act. To the contrary, for this process of inter-generational giving and sharing to work, the parents will want to actively promote the direct interaction of the two generations and will quickly understand that their intervention can only inhibit that process. I do recognize that some adults whose relationships with their parents are unsatisfactory or sadly broken may see no benefit in this practice. They may feel they are putting their children in harm's way to permit this sort of independent interaction with their grandparents. I fully sympathize with their feelings and suggest that in those cases this practice may not be appropriate until the relationship between parent and child is restored.

Seventh, hidden in my description of the grant-making process in the fifth point above are critical life skills. When each grandchild comes forward and makes his or her request, he or she is learning the life skills of public speaking, leadership, and passionately advocating for something on the behalf of others. I cannot begin to count the number of times clients of mine have said how much they wish that as young people they had learned how to overcome their anxieties about public speaking. They wish they had lost their fears of coming into a room of people and asking for something, their inability to prepare an agenda or a proposal, and their inability to successfully advocate a position in which they passionately believed. Think about how much more successful in life we would each be had we learned these skills at an early age. The secret behind grandchild/ grandparent philanthropy is that in making and advocating a grant request, all of these skills are brought into play in an atmosphere of love and caring and with an outcome that benefits not oneself but others. Many of the families I work with have instituted this form of philanthropy and are actively using it to teach and practice these skills. These families understand that if their children are to be ready to take on roles of leadership and governance in or outside of the family, these critical skills are necessary.

Grandchild/grandparent philanthropy enables the participants to learn about one another's passions, give to others, and practice important life skills. For grandparents, it offers an active role in family governance that fully engages their wisdom and their natural love and affection for their grandchildren. For both grandparents and grandchildren, it offers a shared experience of learning about one another while also discovering the world and its needs.

Chapter Notes

1. I am indebted to Daniel J. Boorstin, whose volumes *The Discovers, The Creators,* and *The Seekers* document our species' history.

2. Murray Bowen, *Family Therapy in Clinical Practice.*

3. More on this practice can be found in a separate piece called *"Reflections on Grandchild/Grandparent Philanthropy as an Element in a System of Family Governance"* on the website www.jamesehughes.com and can be downloaded from that site.

Chapter Seven

The Family Bank

THE FAMILY BANK provides a means for a family's wealth to be leveraged by making loans available to family members on terms not available commercially. These are loans that would be considered high risk by commercial bankers but are low risk to the family because of their contribution to the family's long-term wealth preservation plan. Loans from a family bank are usually for two purposes: investment, to increase the family's financial and intellectual capital; or enhancement, to increase the family's intellectual and human capital.

In the case of loans for investment, the family's purpose is to take advantage of opportunities brought by individual family members. The loans afford the family opportunities to grow its financial wealth while enhancing the intellectual growth of individual members. These are frequently investments in businesses founded by individual family members. Such business loans follow these basic rules:

1) The borrower prepares a business plan and a loan application equivalent to that required by any commercial lender.

2) The borrower discusses the project's feasibility with the family bank's board and advisers.

3) When a loan is granted, the borrower provides proper business reports on the investment.

4) The borrower ultimately repays the loan.

This process gives the family borrower excellent business training and the highest possible chance of a successful financial outcome.

Another form of investment loan, as discussed in Chapter 5, is for investor allocation. These are loans from older generation family members to younger generation family members or to the family's long-term trusts to provide capital for investments. Frequently, these are investments in high-risk, high-reward asset classes, such as venture capital, hedge funds, or high-yield bonds. These loans shift the growth of financial assets to the youngest members of the family as part of a long-term wealth preservation strategy.

With enhancement loans, the family's purpose is to increase the family's intellectual and human capital by increasing the independence of individual family members. Many families, and particularly many family trustees, cannot make the intellectual leap between the words "subsidy" and "enhancement." Too often requests for help by family members are treated as requests for subsidization and create dependence on the part of the family members. Dependence on subsidization, or as I call it "dependence on remittance," is an addiction that is as serious as dependence on alcohol or drugs. It saps the human and intellectual capital of a family faster than almost any other single liability on the family balance sheet. As with investment loans, proper lending procedures for enhancement loans are critical to the growth of each borrower's human and intellectual capital. When seeking an enhancement loan, the borrower should be encouraged to state how such a loan will increase his or her independence and how the loan will add to the family's intellectual capital. When a family's leadership begins to view distributions to individual family members as enhancement loans, and family members agree to formally apply to the family bank when seeking such loans, a family makes real progress in combating remittance addiction. When family members explain to their peers and advisers on the family bank board how a particular loan will be enhancing, they must be certain that their individual human and intellectual capital will really be enhanced. With enhancement loans, repayment comes in the form of the increased independence of the individual borrower and his or her increased capital. This idea has a long and fruitful history.

Perhaps the most noted example of successful use of a family bank is that of the Rothschilds, as recounted in Chapter 1. The progenitor of that family, Mayer Amschel Rothschild, provided private banking services to an aristocratic German family and helped them successfully overcome the dislocation in their part of Germany caused by war. His success provided him with significant financial capital. Rothschild was also extremely fortunate to have an abundance of human capital: five sons. (I apologize that eighteenth-century history tells us next to nothing about his daughters.) As you recall, Mayer Rothschild decided to create five new banks, one in each of the then financial capitals of Europe. He asked each of his sons to move to one of these centers and head up the new branch bank. As an incentive, he loaned each son the initial capital for the new branch bank. As a further incentive, he charged a lower rate of interest than an outside lender would have, and he asked for none of the new banks' profits. He wanted each of his sons to become individually successful through the success of his own bank. Finally, he required that the loans be repaid so that future family borrowers would have the means to pursue new opportunities.

This plan alone would likely have served his sons' individual interests. But Mayer Rothschild also understood the importance of intellectual capital in family wealth preservation. And so he required, as additional interest for each loan, that his sons continually advise him of what was happening in their businesses and the financial centers where they were located. This sharing of information gave the Rothschilds a bank of knowledge to use to help one another, and it quickly distanced them from their competitors.

Today the idea of a global business built on intellectual capital is sweeping the world. In the eighteenth century it was unheard of. When we speak of families who have preserved wealth over more than three generations, and even more importantly are still growing, the Rothschild family is one to emulate.

Families striving to preserve their wealth quickly grasp that while having a friendly lender gives an enormous competitive boost, it is the sharing of intellectual capital that is the true wealth-preserving reason for forming a family bank.

A family bank provides a safe environment in which each family member can obtain a financial education. Most schools don't teach people how to obtain a mortgage, a car loan, a personal loan, or a business loan. This deficiency deters most individuals in their financial growth. It also leads most of us to learn by necessity. While this works well for a few people, who are gifted in this field, the system leaves many financially undereducated and ultimately financially unsuccessful. If a family's goal is to enhance the lives of its members, it should ensure that each family member receives a full financial education. The creation of a family bank fosters such an education.

The families I have counseled on wealth preservation have found the family bank useful for providing financial education, a sense of community, character building, and financial mistake-making in a safe environment, all while increasing the family's financial, intellectual, and human balance sheets through the cumulative successes of the individual borrowers.

Here are some guidelines for setting up a family bank.

- The family bank should not be a formal institution. It isn't a bank in the normal corporate sense. It is important that it be informal so that its activities remain private and so that it can evolve a system of governance that meets the unique circumstances of the family that creates it.

- The family bank must have formal rules for meetings. It should have officers, directors, and, if needed, advisory boards. It should have procedures for receiving and processing loan applications. That said, the rules and procedures will vary considerably, depending on who will fund the loans.

- The family bank must have a mission statement explaining its philosophy and reason for being. The lenders and borrowers must understand the family bank's purpose—to be a high-risk, low-interest lender—and the consequences of that policy. The bank's mission statement should also contain a values section incorporating the overall family mission statement and should explain how the bank will assist in carrying out that mission.

- Because family trusts are potential lenders and borrowers, it is particularly important that trustees understand and agree to participate in the family bank. Trustees' involvement in the family bank, as in so many other areas of family governance, points up the need for excellence in their selection.

• It is important to have concurrence of all family members, both lenders and borrowers, with the terms of the bank's mission statement.

• It is particularly important that all family members who agree to participate in the family bank be given copies of all loan applications. Personal financial data may be withheld for confidentiality, but all members should receive the intellectual capital portions of the applications.

Chapter Eight

Protectors, Advisers, Mentors, and *Hommes d'Affaires*

This chapter is dedicated to John O'Neil, mentor of mentors.

IN THIS CHAPTER I will discuss the nature and roles of protectors, advisers, mentors,[1] and *hommes d'affaires,* and how each is helpful in the implementation of a family governance plan.

Protectors

What is a protector, and what role does he or she play in family governance? The legal concept we know as protector originated with trusts drafted principally by counsel in the United Kingdom. Today this concept is used extensively in the United States to solve two serious trust governance problems.

A protector can fill the need for an impartial person who will never have any interest in the income or principal of a trust but has the authority to consent to certain requests by the beneficiary. Frequently, when younger members of families inherit substantial assets, they are unprepared for the responsibility of full control over their financial affairs. This problem occurs most often with distributions to young family members upon the termination of Uniform Gift to Minors Accounts at age eighteen or twenty-one and when trusts terminate and distribute substantial sums. The problem also occurs with the marriages of younger generation family members when gifts are made to help the newlyweds get started, but the donor family wants to preserve these assets for its family member should the marriage fail. In each of these situations, counsel frequently recommends the creation of a revocable trust to hold the funds in question. Counsel also suggests that the young person be a trustee either alone or with someone else so the young person will learn how to manage his or her affairs. Finally, counsel suggests that the young person voluntarily limit his or her right to revoke or amend the trust by requiring the consent to either of these actions of a person in whom he or she has great confidence. The person who has the power of consent is referred to as a protector. This same consenting role is often suggested in the case of elderly family members who are putting assets into trusts for their own protection against senility or undue influence.

A second role for a protector is to represent all of the beneficiaries of a trust in removing the trustee if the beneficiaries request it. In all governance systems checks and balances must be created to ensure that no part of the system can become a law unto itself. All parts of the system must remain accountable to the others. In a family governance system that includes trusts, the family members who are the beneficiaries must have a way to ensure the accountability of their trustees and to remove and replace unsatisfactory trustees.

Few trust agreements prior to the 1980s provided a system for removal of trustees. During the 1980s, as families became more educated about their governance systems, they learned how to measure whether they were receiving excellent service from their trustees. Families discovered, unfortunately, that not all trustees had been performing at a level of excellence, and in such cases sought to replace them. Many families, to their distress, learned from their counsel that unless a trustee voluntarily resigns, he or she is nearly impossible to remove. Although beneficiaries can prove that a trustee has been anything but excellent, most courts will not agree to a trustee's removal unless he or she has committed theft, is an alcoholic or mentally incapacitated, or has acted recklessly. Families also discovered that the trust had to bear the costs of court proceedings to remove a trustee, and that these costs were substantial: hard costs, such as accounting and legal fees for both parties, as well as soft costs, such as the loss of family financial privacy due to the public nature of court proceedings. Clearly, checks and balances were non-existent in this system of trustee/beneficiary governance, from the perspective of a beneficiary seeking excellence from his trustee.

A solution to this governance problem is to put into all family trust agreements provisions for the naming of a protector, provisions that give the beneficiaries the power to request the protector to remove the trustee, and provisions that give the protector the power in his discretion to do so. Some counsels give the power of removal of a trustee directly to the beneficiaries and do not use protectors. At one time there were tax concerns with beneficiaries having this direct power of removal. For the present, these concerns appear to have been overcome. Normally, in matters of governance, I advocate that people act for themselves by taking responsibility for their own affairs. In the case of the power of removal of a trustee, I prefer the interposition of the protector between the trustee and the beneficiary. Why? Because the protector does not have to remove the trustee. The protector can look at the situation dispassionately and, if he or she believes it is in the best interests of the beneficiaries, act as a mediator between the beneficiaries and the trustee—a mediator with a steel hand inside a velvet glove. If the mediation does not work, the trustee knows that the protector can and probably will remove him. The further advantage of this procedure is that it settles disputes between the beneficiaries and the trustee outside the court system. This process saves time and money and, more importantly, maintains the privacy of the family's financial affairs.

Protectors are also helpful when a family is using a private trust company (PTC) as trustee (see Chapter 15). Provisions for a protector in individual trusts can help a family member decide to move his or her existing trusts into a PTC or to use the PTC as the trustee for new trusts. In these cases the protector gives the family member certainty that he can withdraw and change trustees if the PTC proves to be unsatisfactory. Remember, "If you know how to go, you will stay; if you do not know how to go, you will spend your life trying to figure it out."

Protectors are a wonderful addition to a system of family governance. They are an idea whose time has come.

Advisers

How do advisers fit into a system of family governance? In his book, *Creating Effective Boards for Family Enterprises,* John Ward advocates that family businesses have boards of directors. He further suggests that these boards contain strong nonfamily members. I have previously stated my belief that all families are in business—the business of wealth preservation. It will not surprise you that I, therefore, believe that all families should have boards of directors.

Taking John Ward's advice, I suggest that the family use its outside advisers as the nonfamily members of its board of directors. It has always seemed strange to me that I rarely meet most of the other advisers to the families who have asked for my help. Whenever I suggest such a meeting, my client families are delighted, and it happens right away. What I learn from my fellow advisers about the families we are helping gives me insights that I simply would not otherwise get. Family members who attend these meetings are frequently surprised that the whole (all of the advisers) can solve intractable problems, whereas previously the parts (each adviser alone) could find no answer. While each adviser must be selected for his or her special skill, family advisers serving together as the outside members of a family board of directors may well demonstrate their greatest value. In my experience, these meetings, with all advisers present, are nearly always productive. The only time they are not useful is when professional jealousy or defensiveness gets in the way of the work. Bringing a professional facilitator into the first advisers' meeting will avoid this silliness and get all advisers working together from the outset.

Mentors

Mentors form a central part of the teaching cadre of a family. Mentors are people we look up to and respect. We invite them to ask us questions about who we are and who we aren't. They guide us through our journey by challenging our goals, debating our ideas, and helping us deal with failure.

Great mentors, unlike teachers, almost never provide answers. They rather seek to provide their mentees with the questions they believe will best lead to learning by the individual being mentored. A successful mentoring relationship will lead the mentee to discover, through the mentor's art, a *process* of learning that will be unique to him or her and which he or she can use throughout a lifetime. Discovering how you learn, and not how anyone else learns, is the deepest value gained from great mentoring. True mentorship is the expression of wisdom through intuition in guiding someone toward greater self-awareness and freedom in their pursuit of happiness. Successful mentoring is a dialogue in which both parties learn something essential. It must entail joint learning.

Teachers, coaches, elders, and best friends are often mistaken for mentors. Of course, they may act as mentors when called to such a relationship, but their basic roles serve a different purpose. Here are the differences:

1) **Teaching** consists of one person—the teacher—having data and information, and sometimes knowledge, that are sought by another person. The teacher has things to recite and explain to the student, who attempts to memorize and integrate this data and information. This process is rarely very dynamic or experiential—that is, learning through Socratic questioning and case study. In uncommon instances, when the learning comes from the student's questions and experiences, and when the questioning continues until the student feels that she or he has fully integrated the answers, we reach the boundary between teaching and mentoring.

2) **Coaching** consists of one person transmitting specific skills to another who wishes to enhance an area of his or her life. The coach normally uses a special set of skills developed to master a particular practice to train the student. Coaching is always a dynamic interchange between coach and trainee, with the trainee doing most of the work. Coaches don't tailor lessons to each player's learning style; they have a basic system for teaching all who seek their knowledge. The few coaches who can adapt their instruction to nurture the skills of an individual trainee are closer to being mentors.

3) **Eldering** is a relationship with someone to whom we have granted authority over some part of our lives to give us advice and assist us in maturing. We grant them the right to guide us in the correct paths, because we believe that their lives exemplify journeys in which they have been able to learn some of life's secrets. Elders are like mentors in that they ask questions and use story and metaphor to teach. Unlike mentors, they are not proactive and normally have responsibilities toward an entire tribe rather than toward an individual.

4) **Best friends** are normally relationships of the heart. Both parties seek a place in which they can trust the other to keep their secrets and promises and to value each other at the highest level. Best-friend relationships are highly intimate and fundamentally nonhierarchical, and they may last for a lifetime. Although in a mentoring relationship both parties may ask questions and learn from the relationship, a best friend relationship is not mentoring. In the mentoring relationship it is the mentee's questions that form the basis of the dialogue. Mentoring is essentially about the mentee, not about a shared bond.

In order to find a mentor, you must first ask yourself what exactly you are seeking to learn at this stage of your life. Is it a body of knowledge, or is it a deeper understanding of yourself? In other words, are you at a point where you wish to learn more about your intellect and your role in the world—to look outward, from the boundary between teaching and mentoring—or do you wish to look inward, and discover more about your intuition, your interior self?

When you have established the question you wish to answer, the next critical stage in finding a mentor is to begin asking that question of your inner circle, the people you trust the most. The mentor and mentee must always be ready to acknowledge, from the relationship's beginning, that the mentoring relationship is, by nature, temporary. Acknowledging the transitory nature of this relationship at the beginning gives the greatest promise for its successful conclusion.

Mentoring is a calling. When you seek a mentor, seek someone who is called to such a role and, most important, is called to the unique questions of that stage in your life. Be wary of people who suggest they know much. Be attracted to people whom your intuition suggests know much but who themselves profess to know little.

Wise men like John Gardner and Warren Bennis teach that one of the critical components of a happy life is lifelong learning. If a family considers its assets to be its members and sees its mission as aiding each family member in his or her pursuit of happiness, the family is going to need mentors to assist with each member's learning. I believe each family member's résumé should include a list of his or her mentors. I want to be clear: I am not speaking of who the family members' heroes are; I am speaking of the people from whom they are learning. Being without a mentor is like being without a coach when you are trying to learn a sport. You might learn something from a book about the sport, its rules, and maybe even some technique, but when you go out and try to play, you'll fail.

Hommes d'Affaires

Hommes d'affaires serve a family as impartial barometers of their governance system's form and development. They teach families how to set up their government to achieve excellent joint decision making over a long period of time. The *homme d'affaires* guides the family government through its natural evolution, helping to preserve the basic order and core values the family shares, while always subordinating his or her ambition to the service of the family members.

Hommes d'affaires observe and talk to each family member to determine how these multiple personalities coalesce to create the personality of the family. They strive to understand a family's character, its process, and its strengths and weaknesses. By mentoring the family's leaders, the *homme d'affaires* can impart the importance of leadership that enhances the life journey of each family member. Without this kind of guidance, leaders will soon have no one to lead, and the family governance system will fall into chaos.

Hommes d'affaires should offer clients a healthy and loving skepticism about others' behavior. They point out all examples of self-interest. Skepticism about human behavior is not about viewing life through dark, anxious glasses, or seeing humans as fatally flawed. Rather, it is viewing with compassion the truth of the human condition. It is actively supporting each individual's struggle to achieve deep spiritual happiness from a place of humility, while doubting that anyone in this lifetime is going to achieve it. *Hommes d'affaires* bring to the families they serve a deep awareness of human behavior and the truths and consequences that behaviors represent and entail. Often in the families I work with, their financially privileged positions have isolated them from many human interactions. All too frequently, younger members of these families have been abandoned emotionally by their parents and exhibit behaviors associated with abandonment in their interpersonal relationships. They are not prepared for normal human interaction and, in my experience, can easily fall victim to others. The true *homme d'affaires* brings to these clients a worldly-wise view of human behavior and gentle mentoring in the arts of human interaction.

Knowing that the true *homme d'affaires*'s personal journey of service begins with a willingness to subordinate him or herself to the patron, the family's leader permits the patron to accept such a gift without fearing loss of place or competition. A reciprocity of gratitude—one person for being allowed to serve and the other for being served—is the essence of the relationship.

An excellent *homme d'affaires* should have:

1) an interest in the art of governance;

2) a belief in orderly evolutionary change;

3) a skeptical view of human behavior; and

4) a willingness to subordinate ambition to the higher calling of service to another.

Protectors, advisers, mentors, and *homme d'affaires* each have a special role to play in successful family governance. They are the family's outside assets.

Before closing this chapter, I want to add a few thoughts on the issues families face in selecting outside advisers, particularly attorneys. At the present time, the American public holds professionals, and particularly attorneys, in low esteem. As a sixth-generation lawyer, with a seventh, my nephew, working in my office, I am particularly upset about the state of my beloved profession.

To trace how the advisory professions achieved this unenviable reputation is beyond the scope of this book.[2] For families, the key issue is that most professional firms are no longer organized to solve their clients' problems. They are organized to sell products to their clients. Frankly, these firms are no longer professional organizations, they are businesses. I believe that as soon as the professions acknowledge this fact, their reputations will improve, because their new customers (no longer clients) will be able to buy their products at competitive market prices instead of at inflated hourly rates.

As professional firms have evolved into businesses, private-client practices dedicated to family issues have been disappearing. Why? Such practices are uniquely professional. Private-client work cannot be mass-produced; each client's problems must be solved individually. These are tough, messy human problems rather than neat and clean numbers issues. For the businessman-attorney, the goal is to help the customer swallow up the other guy before he swallows you. In private-client work, it is pretty hard to recommend to your client that she swallow her sister.

Another problem private-client advisers have is the feeling that if they are not tax specialists, they will starve for lack of business. These advisers are on the wrong track, because they are serving only the liability side of a family's balance sheet. Taxes don't promote the well-being of family members, the asset side of the balance sheet; they are a cost of a family's doing business. Any entrepreneur knows she has to spend 70 to 80 percent of her time generating revenue or she will go out of business. An adviser serving the cost side of the family balance sheet is on the wrong side of his client's affairs. Tax reduction is important, but taxes have almost nothing to do with twenty-, fifty-, or one-hundred-year planning. The tax rules simply change too often. Taxes are extremely short-term liabilities on a family balance sheet.

Where can private clients find great advisers? Look for contrarians, women and men who have chosen professional paths that are different and who know why they are on those paths. Seek people who describe themselves as "called" to this work. Look for people who are greatly interested in other people, are curious about you, and who are creative in areas beyond their professional lives. Seek a person who might become your friend, your spouse's friend, and your children's friend. After all, you will be working on family governance together for a long time. My father and I are very proud that I'm working with the fourth and fifth generations of families whose first, second, and third generations he served.

Finally, seek advisers with "grasshopper" minds. My first teacher, mentor, and friend in the law, George Farnham, taught his associates that the secret to success in private-client work was the ability to work on fifteen to twenty different problems every day, jumping from one to another like a grasshopper. He felt that you had to have seen an enormous variety of situations before you had enough experience to offer a family any useful advice. He understood how easily the advice he gave could violate the Greek philosopher's injunction to all professionals, "Above all in the advice you give, do no harm" and sought always to avoid such an outcome.

Over the years, I have been blessed by many wonderful colleagues, who have helped my clients immeasurably. The ones who chose private-client work all had four special qualities. They genuinely liked people. They had "grasshopper" minds. They were very long-term thinkers. And they strove above all to "do no harm."

Chapter Notes

1. My complete thoughts on mentoring can be found in Chapter 17.

2. Readers who are interested in the status of the legal profession will learn a great deal from the book *The Betrayed Profession,* by my former partner, Sol Linowitz.

PART THREE

Roles and Responsibilities

Chapter Nine

Control Without Ownership

CONTROL WITHOUT OWNERSHIP expresses a way of thinking, a philosophy. This concept, when practiced, powerfully assists a family to overcome the proverb "Shirtsleeves to shirtsleeves in three generations." Control without ownership means that each family member adopts the idea that "I am the owner of something if I control it, even if I am not the legal owner of that thing."

In the thirty-five years I have practiced law, giving up ownership of anything is the most difficult issue my clients have faced and yet, once done, the most wealth preserving. In the early years of my practice, I noticed that very few older family members made substantial transfers during their lifetimes to younger members, despite the fact that the liabilities that encumbered their family balance sheets could be substantially reduced if they did so. I therefore assumed that people generally had no desire to give anything away. As the years have passed, I have discovered that people are in fact very willing to give up ownership, but not control of decision making. Fear of loss of control is often so profound that it continues to permeate some individuals' planning processes after their deaths. Any of us who practice in this field, or who have closely observed wealthy families, know of estate plans that have attempted to "control from the grave" and left later generations leading dependent and unproductive lives. Every plan for long-term wealth preservation has to take the issue of control into account and find a way to deal with it positively.

Here is an example of how this philosophy works in practice. Some years ago a wealthy individual in his late sixties came to see me for estate planning. The family consisted of his wife, two children, and grandchildren. He had just finished five years of intra-family litigation with a prior generation of family trustees. The experience had been so unsatisfactory to him that he had decided, despite an excellent comprehension of estate tax issues, to leave his entire estate outright one-half to his wife and one-half to his children. After I had taken his instructions, I asked him if he would be willing to give me some information about his family members so I could form an impression of them. What I learned was that his wife, a woman in her sixties, had no formal or informal business education. He paid all the bills and made all the financial decisions. She had siblings who had poor financial histories and were constantly seeking financial assistance from her. His eldest son, just forty, had been divorced once, was in a second "so-so" marriage, and had children from each marriage. His daughter, in her late thirties, was single, a physician, and had already been named in two malpractice claims. Neither claim had resulted in a judgment against her, but the experience had left her frightened. After hearing these facts, I asked him frankly whether he expected the fortune he had worked hard to create and wanted to leave to the people he loved would be preserved or dissipated by his plan. Quite properly, his reaction to my question was to wonder out loud whether it was any of my business and to ask me to get on with preparing the papers he wanted. I think every reader can imagine that had this plan been implemented, it would have been highly unlikely that this family would be financially sound by the time the grandchildren were grown.

Happily, in this case, a week later my client called and asked to see me again. He came in and said, "You asked me a single question; I avoided answering it because I want my wife and children to be in control of their lives, not battling with trustees, but I can see that leaving them the direct ownership of my assets has some real dangers. In my wife's case, I'm sure her relatives will end up with a substantial portion of her property. In my son's case, his second wife may leave him, and the two sets of children aren't friendly. And finally, my daughter's medical practice leaves her financially vulnerable to her patients. How can I leave my family members in control of their financial lives without giving them direct ownership of my assets?" I replied, "Teach them that to control something without legally owning it is the best financial position anyone can ever be in." My client then asked, "Why?" I said, "Let's look at your facts. Your wife has little or no financial education; how would she learn 'on the job' to invest money? How would she find the strength to resist her siblings' requests? What are the odds that she would choose able advisers when she has no experience of doing so? Who would help her to learn investor allocation, to create a family bank, to manage a family balance sheet? The odds against her successfully preserving your fortune will be very high. However, if she is in control of learning how to do these things, with strong representatives she has chosen to guide her, and she doesn't bear the risk of ownership while she is learning, then she has a real chance of wealth preservation. The critical issue is that she learns this concept of control and her role in managing it."

I told him that the same concept offers power to his son and daughter to combat different but equally real risks to their financial futures. My client took that in: "You are right; control without ownership offers my wife, my son, and my daughter powerful help. However," he said, "I have had terrible results with trustees, and I already know you are going to tell me trusts are the answer. What can I do to overcome the problems I see with trusts and with the significant liabilities the individual members of my family face?"

I then explained to him the methods he needed to teach and to use to help his family while mitigating the problems he had previously encountered with trusts. These methods are set forth in the remaining chapters of Part Three. These chapters deal with the questions of empowering beneficiaries, of trustees as representatives of beneficiaries, of peer review, and of private trust companies.

I further commented on the liabilities that would be associated with my client's death, particularly the loss of his knowledge (intellectual capital) that he had not communicated to his wife, and the loss of his strength in assisting her in dealing with her sibling issues—liabilities that put one-half of his fortune at risk. His failure to plan for his son's problems of divorce and mixed-family jealousies and his daughter's exposure to lawsuits put the other half of his fortune at risk.

You will note that my example does not include tax issues. I assume that the long-term tax benefits of trusts are known to most readers and that these advantages will be explained fully by their attorneys, accountants, or other financial planners. Furthermore, I believe that taxes are the most easily handled liability on the family balance sheet.

My example also does not deal with external liabilities, where control without ownership protects against expropriation, exchange control, extortion, and Holocaust. A hostile government can't reach assets you don't own. Whether the liabilities are internal or external, if you control something but don't own it, your chance of successfully managing the wealth-preserving issues posed by a particular liability to your continued use and enjoyment of that thing are improved.

In Chapter 1 I explained that long-term wealth preservation is a process of making slightly more good decisions than bad over a long period of time. In this process of decision-making, you hope to reduce as much as possible the consequences of bad decisions. If you own something and make a bad decision regarding it, the consequences of that decision are immediate. On the other hand, if you control something but don't own it, someone else has to implement your decision. Just the extra time involved in instructing your representatives to implement your decisions may give you the time to see the unforeseen consequence of a decision and to modify it. Just the fact that someone else, whom you trust, is involved in the process offers the real likelihood that your representatives will rapidly implement your best decisions and, perhaps, be a little tardy—as only real representatives should be—in implementing your worst ones.

Some of you may be concerned that any delay could be a negative in our rapidly changing times, when an extra day may mean missing a critical opportunity. Of course, there will be situations when that concern will prove true. On balance, however, when your benchmarks are twenty, fifty, and one hundred years, I believe this extra time helps!

This philosophy, when combined with the practices explained here, removes the need of each family member to have direct owner-ship of all of his or her assets and the accompanying unnecessary exposure to many of the liabilities on the family balance sheet. It also enhances the asset side of a family balance sheet through the individual control it places in the hands of each family member over his or her financial destiny.

Control without ownership is the essence of being a great steward. Control without ownership means I will exercise control over my financial destiny, but I will not put my family's assets at the risk of the liabilities that grow out of my direct legal ownership of those same assets.

Chapter Ten

Beneficiaries

This chapter is dedicated to Joanie Bronfman, my colleague, my friend, and my fellow traveler on the journey to help families govern themselves better.

EVERY YEAR SOMEONE walks through my door who wants to sue her or his trustee. Each has a sad and sometimes horrifying story to tell about what happened to her or him as the beneficiary of a trust. Were the ancestor who created their trust to hear their stories, it is likely that the trust would never have been formed! Why do these stories keep happening when the purpose of a trust is to improve the beneficiary's life? Strangely, as with so much of modern life, the answer as I have experienced it is a paradox. The fundamental problem nearly always lies with the beneficiary and only secondarily with the trustee.

Many readers who have similar stories to tell may now be upset and wondering how the beneficiary can be the problem.[1] In meeting after meeting with aggrieved beneficiaries, I discover that they have never been educated as to what it means to be a beneficiary of a trust. Consequently the roles and responsibilities given to them in that capacity have never been exercised. On what basis can I make such a sweeping statement? Simply that over the thirty-five years of my law practice very few beneficiaries have actually read and understood the terms of the trust of which they are the beneficiary when they first seek my advice. When I participate in seminars on this subject, over and over the participants readily agree that they don't understand their trust documents and, in many cases, have never read them. Clearly, you can't expect good relations in a complex legal relationship if one party to the relationship hasn't even understood her or his basic rights and responsibilities. Frankly, no beneficiary can honestly know if the trustee is or is not performing correctly without understanding the trust instrument.

Throughout this chapter I'll give several examples to prove that failed trustee/beneficiary relations are most frequently initiated by the beneficiary's lack of education on her or his role and responsibility in the relationship. For now, let's turn back to the aggrieved beneficiary in my office and help her start a new process. Her brother is coming in next week, and I'll be teaching him the same things.

After the beneficiary has told her story and explained that she is very angry and wants to sue, I advise her that I don't litigate and that I'll be happy to give her references to a specialist in the field of trust litigation. I do suggest that since she's here, why not discuss the matter with me to see if some course other than litigation might serve her better. Assuming she agrees to keep talking, my first question to her is "Are you an excellent beneficiary?" This is the one question the beneficiary least expects, and after an hour or so with me, the one she wishes I hadn't asked. Why? Because if she decides to try my way of solving the problem through education instead of litigation, she is going to go away from the meeting with lots of homework. Let me quickly add that trustees who act for my client-beneficiaries get lots of homework, too.

Before the meeting is over I'll also explain to her that every well-educated beneficiary demands, and in my experience frequently receives, excellence from her trustee. After all, the trustee is accountable to her, which is something she initially finds hard to comprehend since she was accountable to the trustee for many years. A clear understanding of who is accountable to whom underlies much of the problem in these failed relationships. Once the beneficiary comprehends her roles within the trust and begins to act as a full member in the trustee/beneficiary relationship, these problems often cure themselves.

Lack of beneficiary education leads to another problem, the typical annual trustee's meeting. What's wrong with the typical meeting? First, it's scheduled at 11:15 with lunch to follow at noon. No business meeting takes this format unless it's designed to avoid real work. Second, the meeting consists of an overview of trust accounts. These accounting statements are usually well prepared, correct, and have cost the trust substantial fees to create. Unfortunately, the beneficiary rarely has had a financial education and even more rarely a fiduciary accounting education, and so doesn't have any way to comprehend them. To avoid the embarrassment of admitting that she doesn't understand the statements, and further, being well-bred and wanting not to "waste the trustee's time in teaching," the beneficiary accepts the accounts as prepared. There will then normally be an investment presentation, again, well-prepared and, again, of little use unless the beneficiary has had an investment education. Lunch will then be served, and all possible useful work will conclude. As this is the only experience the trustee and beneficiary have of each other, the likelihood of future problems in their relationship is very high, especially when, at some point in the trust's life, one of the liabilities on the family balance sheet (see Chapter 4) presents itself, and the two parties face that problem with no real ability to talk to each other.

A properly educated beneficiary will change this whole picture. How? First, the annual trustee's meeting will begin at 9 and conclude at 10:30. If the parties want to have a social lunch, that's fine, but not in conjunction with the trust business meeting. Second, the beneficiary will receive the trust accounting to review two weeks before the meeting. The accounting information will be accompanied by a proposed meeting agenda and specific questions from the trustee. Third, a week before the meeting, the beneficiary will adjust the agenda to put the issues she wishes to discuss first and will add specific questions to the trustee. Now a real business meeting will take place: important issues will be addressed, strategic planning will occur, and, most important, the beneficiary and the trustee will be carrying out the roles and responsibilities imposed by their relationship. Later, when family balance sheet liabilities occur, the beneficiary and trustee will have some common experience of working together. They will know who bears the responsibility for solving the problem confronting them and, more importantly, who does not. They will know where the boundaries of their relationship lie so they will understand the capacity of their relationship to solve the problem. Given each family member's need to make the time spent on long-term wealth preservation as productive as possible, think of the extraordinary amount of time wasted by a non- or under-educated beneficiary.

Another issue stemming from lack of beneficiary education occurs within the system of governance I suggest families adopt, the republic (see Chapter 1). A republic assumes an educated electorate who will choose its representatives with care and will hold those representatives accountable when they come back and report the actions taken to fulfill the responsibilities they were elected to carry out.

How pervasive is this education issue? Most readers will be surprised that this isn't just an issue for members of wealthy families who are the beneficiaries of family trusts that last for many generations. Today, most middle-class families have members who also are the beneficiaries of trusts through their participation in tax deferral and savings plans such as ERISA, IRA, 401(k), and other forms of trust arrangements. Whether it's a family of privilege or a middle-class family, these families all have in common the fact that they have chosen trustees to carry out representative governance functions. Each of these families assumes that the beneficiaries will see the trustees as representatives in a relationship of governance that is described as a republic. Unfortunately, very few really understand the role of the beneficiary/voters in a system of trust governance. Even fewer understand the responsibility of the beneficiary/voters to hold their representatives, the trustees, accountable. By accountable I mean in a positive sense of excellence, I don't mean in the negative sense of theft or fraud or gross neglect. The beneficiary is entitled to have an excellent trustee, not just a mediocre-but-legally-correct trustee. If the beneficiary is uneducated about her role in this system of governance, it isn't surprising that the system fails.

As discussed in Chapter 1, history teaches us that when the system of governance in a republic fails, it decays to a pure democracy (or what we understand today as an anarchy) and ultimately to a tyranny or dictatorship. It is not overstating the metaphor of governance to say that the beneficiary who arrives in my office for the first meeting most frequently describes her relationship with the trustee as a tyranny in which she is the person being tyrannized. In governance, as in all relationships, we get out of it what we put into it. Without educated beneficiaries there is a high probability of the relationship's evolving into anarchy at best and into tyranny at worst, even though the tyrant may be a highly benevolent despot.

Hopefully these examples have brought into focus the essential challenges in the trustee/beneficiary relationship. I have carefully avoided discussion here of the issues of dependence and/or entitlement that trusts may create and the human damage that can result from such an unsatisfactory relationship, because I feel others with psychological training have already written on these issues with great thoughtfulness and compassion. Clearly the trust agreement is neutral and doesn't create such a relationship. It is the failure of the parties to the trust agreement to play the roles and assume the responsibilities that the trust agreement properly anticipates that causes the failure of their relationships.

How can we change this situation? The rest of this chapter sets out a scheme that I use to educate a beneficiary and to measure her or his success in achieving excellence. These are subjects that people with a moderate general education can learn. They are designed for people whose journeys in life do not include professional activity in any of the financial professions. These are the family members most at risk of failed relationships with trustees and thus those most at risk of weakening the family's overall governance system.

The set of beneficiary roles and responsibilities on page 108 is being used as a template for learning by many beneficiaries. In my practice it has already proven its worth by changing charged relations between beneficiaries and trustees. It has given both parties a way to measure each other's commitment and willingness to participate in a successful relationship. When the above list is combined with the reciprocal list—trustees' roles and responsibilities, discussed in Chapter 11—the beneficiary understands her or his role in relation to the trustee, often for the first time. Each beneficiary has, by vir-

ROLES AND RESPONSIBILITIES OF BENEFICIARIES

Each beneficiary has an obligation to educate himself or herself about the duties of a beneficiary, as well as the duties of the family trustees. Here are specific responsibilities of beneficiaries:[2]

- To gain a clear comprehension of each trust in which the beneficiary has an interest and a specific understanding of the mission statement for each trust as prepared by the trustees
- To educate himself or herself about all trustee responsibilities
- To understand the trustee's responsibility to maintain the purchasing power of the trust's capital while maintaining a reasonable distribution rate for the income beneficiaries
- To have a general understanding of modern portfolio theory and the formation and process of asset allocation
- To recognize and look for proof that each trustee represents all beneficiaries
- To meet with each trustee once each year to discuss his or her personal financial circumstances and personal goals and to advise the trustee of his or her assessment of the trustee's performance of the trustee roles and responsibilities to the trust, to the beneficiary, and to family governance
- To become knowledgeable about the functions and importance of each element of the family's trust governance structure
- To attend the annual family business meeting and to accept responsible roles within the family governance structure, based on his or her qualifications for such roles
- To develop a general capacity to understand fiduciary accounting
- To demonstrate a willingness to participate in educational sessions and to become financially literate (through family seminars and family-funded educational programs)
- To know how and in what amount trustees and other professionals are compensated and to obtain a general understanding of the budgets for the trust and investment entities in which the trust will be invested

tue of the list of trustee roles and responsibilities, a way to evaluate how well her or his trustees are fulfilling their duties, and with this knowledge each beneficiary becomes an educated consumer. She or he can now take a proper place in trust governance. She or he can now understand how "control without ownership" works and why it's so helpful. She or he can finally begin to appreciate the gift the founder of the trust intended when the trust was created and how privileged she or he is to have received such a gift.

Chapter Notes

1. I am not suggesting that trustees aren't part of the problem, because they are, and in the next chapter of this book I'll discuss their roles and responsibilities in family governance.

2. I am indebted to Richard Bakal, who assisted me in the development of these criteria.

Chapter Eleven

Trustees

This chapter is dedicated to Richard Bakal, the deepest student of the relationship between beneficiaries and trustees I know.

TWO COMPLEX RELATIONSHIPS are formed between a beneficiary and a trustee when a trust is created. First is the legal relationship, and the resulting individual and joint responsibilities created by that relationship. Second is the behavioral dynamic between a beneficiary who is fully educated on what it means to be a beneficiary, and a trustee who understands that his or her role is to be the beneficiary's representative.

In Chapter 10, I related the many times a beneficiary has entered my office wanting to get rid of a trustee. In this chapter, it is my goal to help trustees understand how to excel at what they do so that no beneficiary will ever come into my office, or anyone else's, asking for their removal. I must pause here to apologize to the trust litigation bar for "taking the bread out of their mouths."

I have a second goal far more important to successful family governance: that the relationship between the beneficiary and the trustee be so smooth that each sees himself as an equal member of a team working for a common goal of long-term family wealth preservation. To achieve this goal, the trustee must clearly understand who the beneficiary is as an individual and must want to promote her or his pursuit of happiness. The beneficiary, equally, must fully appreciate the legal realities under which the trustee operates; especially the general constraints imposed by the law governing the trust and the specific constraints imposed by the trust agreement. When a beneficiary and a trustee fully appreciate each other's roles and responsibilities in the governance of the trust, their understanding advances the family's long-term wealth preservation plan by making joint governance of the trust a positive experience for both parties. Their successful relationship proves to each of them, and by example to other family members, the utility of "control without ownership," as discussed in Chapter 9, to the achievement and successful practice of long-term family wealth preservation. The problem is that all too often in the beneficiary's eyes, the control and ownership have both resided with the trustee. Now is the time to change this dynamic by educating both parties on their roles and responsibilities in this complex relationship and then practicing the lessons learned.

Even when these roles and responsibilities are understood and accepted by both parties, they are only the structure for the relationship the parties will share. Rarely do the trustee and beneficiary understand that the human relationship they are beginning will be far more important to the trust's success than the proper maintenance of their legal relationship.

Human beings believe that if they are going to give up any part of their freedom of action, the reward for doing so must be of greater value than the loss of freedom it requires. It is the right to choose the party to the new relationship that makes the giving up of freedom possible. Since the beginning of the use of trusts in the Middle Ages, however, very few, if any, beneficiaries have chosen their trustees. Founders, grantors, settlers—whatever term we use—select the trustees of the trusts they create.

When we understand that the relationship between the trustee and the beneficiary is an arranged marriage of sorts, it's natural that some beneficiaries will feel unheard, misunderstood, or poorly represented by the chosen trustee. The trustee and the beneficiary are often strangers to one another when they are thrust into a relationship that could last a lifetime. Regardless of personal situations or opinions, the grantor has entrusted great responsibilities to both parties, in faith that they will work together to keep the trust solvent. To ensure the long-term health of the trust, they both must accept a difficult challenge: the beneficiary to educate him or herself to an acceptable level of competence in trust management, and the trustee to guide and facilitate that education.

Beneficiaries may only achieve excellence in their role (as discussed in Chapter 10) when trustees look past their position as mere administrators and accept the deeply challenging role of mentor.[1] With guidance, education, and encouragement the beneficiary will grow empowered to accept full responsibility for his or her role in the relationship, culminating in the evolution of the trustee from mentor to representative.

When the trustee and the beneficiary make joint decisions, and the beneficiary has become an equal party to the representative system of governance, the trustee will almost never have to exercise a deciding vote. The beneficiary will know that even if the trustee makes a decision with which she or he disagrees, the trustee's view, acting as her or his representative, is likely to be a fair one.

When selecting a trustee, the grantor of a trust will be well advised to consider the potential trustee's ability to mentor the beneficiaries he or she loves as the highest qualification among all of the things a trustee must do. If a trustee is an excellent administrator, a superb and prudent investor, and a Solomonic and humane distributor but is perceived by the beneficiary to be distant, aloof, and unable to communicate in a way the beneficiary can understand, their relationship will surely be unsuccessful. Unless the trustee accepts a role as the beneficiary's mentor and ultimate representative, the trust may never achieve the success the grantor had hoped for when she or he created it to help lead to the beneficiary's individual pursuit of happiness.

What are a trustee's legal roles and responsibilities? First, a trustee is a fiduciary who owns something given to him by another and who owes that person or another person a duty to care for that thing as if it were his own. A fiduciary can't do anything with that thing to benefit himself. A fiduciary carries the highest duty of trustworthiness imposed by the law. A fiduciary has a duty, after a period of time, to return the thing he holds to the person who put it into his hands, or to someone else if that is what the original person who gave it to him directs, with the thing being in equal or better condition than when he received it.

A trustee is a type of fiduciary who has been given something to hold by one party, called the grantor, for a stated period of time for the benefit of a second party, called the beneficiary. Sometimes the beneficiary is also the person who gave the thing to the trustee.

A historical and helpful example of the trustee-beneficiary relationship comes to us from the time of the Crusades. Let's imagine a knight about to go off to the Holy Land to fight for Christianity. The knight is on his horse and is saying goodbye to his wife and ten-year-old son. The knight looks out over his land and hopes his son will one day inherit it from him. The knight then notices his neighbor and remembers that his neighbor is not going to join him in the Crusade. He then begins to wonder: Suppose I die in the Holy Land? Who will protect my wife and my son from my neighbor's taking my land? Happily the local bishop has just arrived to give his blessing to the knight and to thank him for going on the Crusade. The knight then asks the bishop if the bishop would be willing to hold the title to his land while he is away on the Crusade. He explains to the bishop that if he returns, he will expect the bishop to return the title to him, and that if he does not return, he will expect the bishop to hold the title until his son reaches his majority and then to turn the title over to his son. Finally, he also asks the bishop to keep his neighbor on the neighbor's side of the boundary while he is away. The bishop, happy that the knight is about God's work, agrees that in return for the knight's willingness to go on Crusade he, the bishop, will carry out the knight's wishes exactly as the knight requests. The bishop becomes a trustee when he receives the land title from the knight. The knight and the knight's son become beneficiaries of a trust at the same moment the bishop becomes a trustee. The agreement between the knight and the bishop constitutes the trust.

Although many families have relied upon trusts for the purpose of managing and disposing of their wealth, the most successful ones understand that the term of a trust represents a period of regency[2] within the representative governance system created by the family. Traditionally, the term "regency" has been used to describe a period during which a king, or other leader, is unable to rule due to minority, prolonged absence (as in the previous example), or a disability such as mental incompetence. A trust is essentially a period of regency, because it represents a time during which full ownership of property is suspended. During this interval of suspension of ownership, the trustee takes possession of property from the prior owner and holds the property for the benefit of the beneficiaries, who at some point—or at several points over a period of time, as set forth in the trust agreement—will become the next owners of such property. The regent must know when to relinquish power and how to effectively transfer it to the rightful beneficiaries. A regent should not, indeed cannot, overstay his or her welcome as the surrogate leader. Even if the trust provisions do not provide a specific moment at which full ownership and control of the property is to be transferred over to the beneficiaries, the trustee must be willing to admit when it is time to hand over power, usually to the beneficiaries but sometimes to a successor trustee who is more suited to the task.

The trustee must discuss carefully with the beneficiaries the logistics of transferring the property, and in what form they wish to receive it. Comprehending the trustee's role as mentor, and the trust's characteristic as a period of regency, brings the reality of this complex legal arrangement into clearer focus for trustee and beneficiary alike. Too often, the trustee is seen only as the prudent investor, competent administrator, and humane distributor. There is no doubt that these trustee functions are important, and if not performed excellently will lead to negative consequences for the trust and its beneficiaries. However, even if these functions are performed with brilliance, a trustee's failure to understand himself as mentor and the trust as a period of regency will lead to a failure to realize the ultimate goal of developing the beneficiaries for eventual ownership of the trust assets.

Now that we're clear on what a trust, a trustee, and a beneficiary are, what specifically do trustees do in carrying out the terms of the trust? A trustee does three things: administers the trust property; invests the trust property; and distributes the trust property, all in accordance with the terms of the trust agreement and with the local laws governing trusts in the place where the trust is administered.

Administration of the Trust

Administration of the trust property means keeping the assets safe. Often this includes employing a custodian to hold securities; collecting the trust income each year; doing the trust's banking; keeping proper books and records of the trust's financial position; preparing and filing the trust's tax returns; and reporting on the trust's financial condition to the beneficiaries. While my description of the trustee's administrative function is very short compared to my description of the investment and distribution functions, don't assume it is less important. In fact, if the administrative function is not performed with equal excellence, the three-legged stool of trustee functions will collapse, upsetting the relationship between the trustee and the beneficiary just as quickly and with as profoundly unsatisfactory results for family governance as would the inadequate performance of either of the other two functions.

Investment of the Trust

Each trust has a specific purpose that brought it into being. The grantor expresses that purpose through the terms he writes into the trust agreement. Typically, the trust has as its purpose the provision of funds for the current needs of a group of people, called the income beneficiaries, over an extended period of time, and then the passing of those funds to a later generation. This later group of people is called the remaindermen.

Trusts created for this purpose create an investing dilemma for the trustee.[3] You will recall that when I defined what a trustee did, I said that among the trustee's responsibilities is the duty to turn over the property in the trust to the remaindermen in as good or better condition than he received it. When a trustee invests the trust's assets, the trustee faces a dilemma since, in addition to preserving the trust's assets, he or she must produce a reasonable current amount of income for the income beneficiaries. In almost every trust, the income beneficiaries would like more income, which, as discussed below, reduces the trustee's ability to grow the trust's assets. The remaindermen want the trust's assets to grow so that when the trust comes to an end, the value of what they receive will be greater. The trustee's decisions on how to invest the trust are governed by his attempts to resolve this dilemma.

A trustee investing to produce the highest amount of current income traditionally buys bonds. Bonds are a form of investment in which the investor, called the lender, lends his money to someone else, called the borrower, who agrees to pay the lender a fixed rate of interest for a period of time and then, at the end of that period of time, to repay the loan. Normally, the borrower owns property of greater value than the amount he's borrowing and agrees that if he doesn't have enough cash to repay the lender when the time comes, the lender can have this property to repay the remaining portion of the loan. This property is called collateral. This form of investment traditionally has been considered lower risk than other forms of investment, such as investments in the stock or equity market.[4]

The trustee's dilemma when he invests in bonds held to maturity is that the value of the principal doesn't grow, and the trustee has to contend with inflation. In modern times high rates of inflation have meant that unless the value of a trust's property is growing, inflation will reduce the purchasing power of the property in the trust. In other words, even though arithmetically the value of the trust remains the same, the purchasing power of the assets is constantly diminishing. Trust law requires that a trustee maintain the purchasing power of the trust's assets during the time he is acting as trustee. Today, if a trustee invests only for current income, he will not be able to return to the remaindermen property whose purchasing power is equal to or greater than the value of the property the trustee originally received. If a trustee fails to meet this standard of investment care, the remaindermen can hold him financially responsible and ask the trustee to make up their loss in value from his own fortune.

Continuing with the trustee's dilemma, let's suppose the trustee decides instead to invest in stocks. A stock investment represents the ownership of an undivided portion of the assets of a corporation that is equal to the proportion of the number of shares owned by the trust to the total number of outstanding shares of the corporation. These shares of stock are subject to the liabilities of the corporation, including specifically its bonds and other borrowings. Normally trustees purchase shares of corporations that offer their stock to investors on a public stock exchange. This is done so that the trust's stock investments can easily be sold when the trustee feels it is desirable to do so. Historically stocks have grown in value and made it possible for a trustee to return to the remaindermen, at the end of the trust, assets of equal or greater purchasing power than those the trustee originally received.

The problem for the trustee here is that investments in stock normally produce, in the form of dividend distributions of a portion of the annual earnings of the corporation, substantially less annual income than do bonds. As the trustee increases the trust's investment in stock, instead of complaints from remaindermen about lack of growth in the trust's assets, the trustee hears from the income beneficiaries that they aren't receiving enough income each year to take care of their needs. The trustee finds himself wishing for the wisdom of Solomon in trying to balance the competing desires of the income beneficiaries and the remaindermen.

Truly there is no clear answer to the trustee's investment dilemma. All the trustee can do is recognize his dilemma and do his best to invest the trust with as high a degree of fairness to both interests as possible. Often when I explain this dilemma to the new generation of a family, they ask me why anyone would ever act as a trustee when he has to balance the desires of all of these human beings, none of whom is likely to be satisfied, and at the risk of his personal fortune if he fails. That is a thought-provoking question.

Distribution of the Trust

The trustee has the responsibility to distribute the income earned by the trust and the assets representing the principal of the trust in accordance with the terms of the trust agreement. Many trusts grant the trustee substantial discretion in determining when, and whether, to make income distributions. This is the issue that provides the greatest possibility for disagreement between the trustee and the beneficiaries. Some trust agreements require the trustee to pay all of the income received by the trust each year to the income beneficiaries. This form of trust is often referred to as a simple trust. Other trusts give the trustee the responsibility of deciding whether to distribute to the income beneficiaries all, some, or none of the income received by the trust each year. This form of trust is often referred to as a complex or discretionary trust. When the trustee is asked to make a decision on distribution, it's called an exercise of discretion.

In addition to distributions of income, most trusts give the trustee the power to distribute, at his or her discretion, part or the entire principal of the trust to the income beneficiaries, and often to the remaindermen as well. The trust agreement normally explains to the trustee what kinds of things the grantor feels the trustee should consider when the trustee receives a request from a beneficiary for a distribution of principal. When a trustee makes a distribution from the principal of the trust after exercising his discretion, it's called an invasion of principal. In addition to discretionary distributions of principal, the trust agreement often directs the trustee to pay a percentage of the principal of the trust to a specific beneficiary when that beneficiary attains a certain age. This form of distribution is called a partial termination of the trust.

Friction between the trustee and beneficiary often arises when the beneficiary makes a request for a discretionary distribution and the trustee determines that such an exercise of discretion is either not permitted by the terms of the trust or is not in the beneficiary's best interest. Necessarily the beneficiary will be upset when his or her request is turned down. In my experience, if the beneficiary is excellently fulfilling his or her roles and responsibilities as beneficiary, as explained in Chapter 10, and is holding the trustee accountable for excellence in accordance with the roles and responsibilities for trustees, as set out later in this chapter, the likelihood of ever facing a turndown is very small. When the beneficiary and trustee are educated about each other's roles and responsibilities and are actively carrying out the duties their relationship imposes, requests will be well received. After all, if a trustee understands that he represents the beneficiary, having been selected as her or his representative by the grantor in accordance with excellent trustee selection practices, why would the trustee and beneficiary not find common cause?

Now that we know what a trustee is and we know what a trustee does, what are the trustee's roles in a dynamic system of family governance?

First, the trustee is an important member of the family's governance structure. Often family trusts will have terms, or "lives," of one hundred years or more and therefore are the family's longest-living members. The trustee's management over the years—measured by the excellence of the trust's administration, its successful investment performance, and its humane distribution programs—will play a significant part in the success or failure of the family's long-term preservation plan. In their management of trusts, trustees act as role models for family members on how best to achieve family wealth-preservation goals.

Second, the trustee is often an owner-in-trust of a substantial part of the financial assets on the family financial balance sheet. In this role, the trustee must coordinate the investment activities of his trust with the activities of all other family members. As an example, the trustee can be critical to the success of investor allocation. The trustee holds the family's longest-term assets and, therefore, can be the most farsighted of all family investors. The trustee must be included in investor allocation so the full potential of the process can be achieved. The trustee must coordinate his investment program with the overall family investment program.

Third, the trustee is best situated to offer long-term family balance sheet education to family beneficiaries. As discussed in this chapter and the previous chapter, it's in the trustee's best interest to have a highly educated beneficiary who can appreciate the extraordinary complexity of the trustee's role. As a mentor, the trustee will spend a lifetime working with a beneficiary and can best transmit to future generations the essence of the family mission statement through excellent family governance practices. The trustee can have an extraordinarily positive influence on the life of a beneficiary, and thus on the whole family balance sheet, when the trustee puts at the core of their relationship his role as the beneficiary's representative. The trustee can be an equally negative force when the trustee begins to believe he alone knows what's best for the beneficiary. This blatant act of hubris by the trustee, acting as tyrant, has destroyed many families. A family governance plan based on a representative form of governance cannot abide a tyrant. The role of trustee as educator, historian of the family mission statement, and mentor is critical to family governance. A trustee, to avoid hubris, must never forget that while he is the owner of the trust assets for a period of time, he is an owner as the representative of the grantor and beneficiaries. He must never forget that he is a fiduciary.

Now that we know what a trustee is and what a trustee does and what the trustee's roles are in family governance, how do we measure a trustee's performance of his multiple roles? The measurement takes place on three different levels within a well-managed family governance plan. First, a well-educated beneficiary, using the roles and responsibilities for trustees outlined in the last part of this chapter, will be able to judge whether a trustee is achieving excellence. Second, I believe that to ensure fairness, there must be a system for outside participation in the measurement of trustee excellence (I will address this more fully in Chapter 14, Peer Review). Third, a protector can create an alternative dispute-resolution mechanism when beneficiaries and their trustees have significant disagreements on the trustee's performance (see Chapter 8, Protectors, Advisers, Mentors, and *Hommes d'Affaires*).

These three techniques provide the necessary checks and balances within a family governance plan to insure that a trustee's performance will be judged fairly by the trust's beneficiaries and by the entire family. These techniques further insure that the trustee is given the necessary room for the exercise of discretion so important to the practice of "control without ownership" in the most responsible way.

The multiple roles and complex responsibilities of trustees are extraordinarily difficult to carry out with excellence, especially over the long periods of time that families need to govern themselves to achieve long-term wealth. The risks that a trustee will fail to be a good representative, or worse yet will become a time-servers, or worst of all will be guilty of assuming that he or she knows better than anyone else, are real risks. The fundamental issue for families is how to gain the enormous long-term benefits of "control without ownership" that come from trusts while avoiding the risks of trustee lassitude leading to entropy and, finally, to chaos.

One possible method for avoiding this trap is to build into trust agreements a process for trustee reaffirmation every five years. If we believe in representative government for long-term family governance, why not ask our trustees to offer themselves for periodic reaffirmation, like all other representatives in a republic? There are now families in the United States who have implemented this plan for reaffirmation of trustees. When they adopted this system, some of the families had long-term irrevocable trusts that had neither contemplated this idea nor could be amended to incorporate it. The currently enfranchised trustees simply decided that if the family beneficiaries wanted a system for change of trustees (representatives), they were entitled to have it. The trustees voluntarily put themselves up for reaffirmation and agreed that if a vote of the beneficiaries didn't endorse them for a new term, they would resign.

Carrying this idea for a trustee reaffirmation system further, all of the corporations in America that offer their services as trustees and that follow best practices have affirmative resignation policies written into the brochures describing their policies and practices to prospective clients. I'm frequently surprised when, in trusts created many years before the adoption of these enlightened policies, the beneficiary requests the selection of a new trustee following a corporate trustee's admitted poor-to-unsatisfactory performance, and the beneficiary discovers that these policies don't seem to apply. Why, I wonder, would any trustee, individual or corporate, want to be the trustee for a beneficiary who has said in good faith, "You have not represented me properly, and I wish to select someone else"? Even if the beneficiary doesn't have all of the correct information about the trustee's performance, how can they be in a representative relationship based on trust if the basic trust isn't present between them?

I believe that many families could strengthen their family governance practices by implementing a trustee reaffirmation system. I appreciate that being an excellent trustee probably won't win any trustee a popularity contest, and that there is, therefore, a risk of mobocracy in the reaffirmation process. I believe this risk to be very small if the family governance plan contains a family mission statement, a family balance sheet, beneficiaries who are educated to carry out their roles and responsibilities, a peer review of trustees, and a system of alternative dispute resolution that employs the wisdom of long-term trust practitioners acting either as protectors or as the outside members of a family board of directors. I believe trusts are an essential part of long-term family governance if a family is to preserve its wealth over a long period of time. Trusts need not disempower people; they have every reason to empower people, but they need to have systems of representative governance to assure the achievement of that purpose.

I am a trustee of many trusts. I believe that being an excellent trustee is the most complex role in any field of financial or political life. Like one of the representations of the Hindu God Shiva, you need six hands. On one hand, you have the grantor's mission for the trust to manage and to explain to the beneficiaries; on the next hand, the income beneficiaries' needs for financial help and education; on the next hand, the remaindermen's goals; on the next hand, the complexity of the modern investment markets; on the next hand, the task of managing the federal, state, and local tax affairs of the trust; and on the sixth hand, of the challenge of understanding trust law and the court system that administers it.

If acting as a trustee is a solitary business fraught with personal financial risk, why, as my new generation of beneficiaries asked, would anyone do it? Because when people you deeply care about want to try to preserve their family member assets and values long into the future, the journey with them is too exciting to say no.

ROLES AND RESPONSIBILITIES OF TRUSTEES

Each trustee has an obligation to educate himself or herself on the duties of a trustee, as well as on the duties of the trust beneficiaries.

The trustee's specific duties are as follows:

- To be fully aware of the grantor's original purposes in creating the trust and the current purposes of the trust, if these have changed over time
- To guide his or her decisions by these purposes
- To act so that the actual operation of the trust is empowering to the beneficiaries, within the provisions of the trust
- To put mechanisms in place to increase the level of financial awareness of the beneficiaries, and to see that such financial education of the beneficiaries is carried out effectively
- To meet at least annually with each beneficiary in order to renew the beneficiary's understanding of the trust, as well as to obtain from each beneficiary full information, financial and otherwise, about his or her personal situation
- To educate himself or herself about all beneficiary responsibilities
- To evaluate and advise each beneficiary on how well he or she is meeting the roles and responsibilities of a beneficiary
- To implement effectively the trust's general policies and procedures as they relate to the following:
  1) the trust's investment goals and acceptable risks,
  2) the selection and/or provision of investment advice and management to accomplish such investment goals within the given risks,
  3) the trust's tax position and the selection of tax services, and
  4) the trust's legal position and the selection of legal services

Chapter Notes

1. My complete thoughts on the trustee as mentor can be found in Chapter 19.

2. My complete thoughts on the trustee as regent can be found in Chapter 20.

3. Well-educated investors will understand that I have enormously simplified the investment process to illustrate the investment function of the trustee. Please carry on this discussion at higher and higher levels in your families.

4. Many investors use the word "equity" to mean the same thing as "stock." In this chapter I use the word "stock," as it is the more common term.

Chapter Twelve

Family Philanthropy

This chapter is dedicated to Peter Karoff, founder of the Philanthropic Initiative; Peggy Dulaney, founder of Synergos; Tracy Gary, founder of The Women Donors Network and of Resourceful Women; and Robert and Wendy Graham, founders of Kataysis and Namaste. Each, in a special way, opened my eyes.

IN THIS CHAPTER I discuss the role of philanthropy in a family governance structure. I will demonstrate how philanthropy can powerfully assist a family in shaping its values and how, through its organization and practice, philanthropy can teach a family how to govern itself.

Philanthropy is first, perhaps, the fundamental parent expression of personal and family values. If the family mission statement is an expression of these values, philanthropy is often the best way to move them into practice. Philanthropy can often be a means for family members who are isolated from society by their wealth to connect with the larger issues of the world and to find an active and meaningful place in it. Philanthropy, or in the original Greek *philos anthropos,* means love of my fellow man. The practice of philanthropy by a family offers its members the opportunity to give to the outside world a portion of their time (human capital), talent (intellectual capital), and money (financial capital). Giving, as all of us know, feels good. Every spiritual tradition has a proverb to remind us of how good it feels. The one I like best is "The world loves a cheerful giver." Every spiritual tradition requires of its adherents that those with more give to those with less. As examples, tithing is a principal responsibility in the Jewish, Islamic, and Christian traditions, and taking care of the poor a principal obligation of most

Eastern religions. Regardless of responsibility, philanthropy is fun.

American society has been blessed by the willingness of American families of privilege to give back substantial parts of their wealth for the betterment of mankind. The Astors, Carnegies, Fords, S. C. Johnsons, Kelloggs, Mellons, Morgans, Pews, and Rockefellers are some of the best-known philanthropic names of fortunes founded in the nineteenth and early twentieth centuries. All have generously and thoughtfully given away, in infinitely varied ways, vast portions of their wealth out of love for their fellow man. In the more recent past, the Annenbergs, Feeneys, Gettys, Hugheses (not relatives), MacArthurs, Milkens, Olins, Packards, and Sacklers have all given enormous sums to endow new philanthropies. Looking toward the future, the Gateses and Buffetts have said they will leave their fortunes to philanthropy. These families understand that philanthropy improves the lives of all of us and, more important, improves the lives of their family members.

These philanthropists were and are wealth preservers to the core. I am always impressed, when I speak to later-generation members of the old families, by the pride expressed when they discuss the extraordinary philanthropic work done by their ancestors. These family members also express great pride in the financial acumen of their forbears and appreciation for the financial benefits that have accrued to them as a result. There is, however, a special lilt to their voices when philanthropy is discussed. Many of the later-generation family members have continued the philanthropic work of their ancestors, albeit in fields of activity that their ancestors could not have imagined and, in some cases, would not have approved. The important thing is that family values of stewardship and giving back were inculcated in the family value system. Even more important, they are active values, calling for family members to participate in the world by sharing their human and intellectual capital and, where appropriate, their financial capital.

While gifts of financial and intellectual capital are important, it is the gift of human capital that is key to the use of philanthropy as a tool for long-term family wealth preservation. It is the sharing of self that makes philanthropy a critical contributor to the preservation of the human assets on the family balance sheet. Work, whether or not for wages, is an important part of feeling useful. In many European and Asian cultures, society is seen as having an obligation to provide useful work to all of its members. American culture, unfortunately, has never subscribed to this ancient humane social and business ethic. These older cultures understand that work is an important element in achieving a healthy life. All families understand how important it is that each of their members work. Philanthropic work meets this need for many family members. Unfortunately, our society at its most mercenary often fails to value philanthropic work at the same level as work for profit. Whenever I encounter this opinion, I refer to Andrew Carnegie's famous essay on philanthropy, or to the writings on philanthropy of the Jewish mystic Maimonides. Anyone who has read these two sources finds that giving, done well, is extraordinarily difficult work. Families must resist the market's short-term view of the value of different kinds of work in favor of the long-term proof of the value of their ancestors' philanthropic work.

Where does philanthropy fit in a family governance structure?

1) Every family mission statement should have a section dealing with the family's responsibility to the outside world and a section on how it will interact with the outside world. How can a family derive a statement of family values that does not include the importance of giving to others less fortunate than itself, or that does not define philanthropy as one of the values the family will project into the world as a symbol of its strength, its "differentness"?

2) Every family balance sheet should reflect the portion of the family's human assets, intellectual assets, and financial assets devoted to philanthropy. How can a family measure the growth of its overall wealth without also showing the growth of the portion of its wealth dedicated to philanthropy?

3) Every family with financial assets in excess of $2 million should create a formal organization to support its philanthropy. The form of organization should be determined in consultation with skilled advisers but, at a minimum, should include a broad structure that will allow participation in decision making by all family members. Families with less than $2 million in financial assets can organize themselves to do philanthropy together without incurring the administrative costs of a formal organization by using a form of philanthropic organization called a *donor advised fund.* Families of substantial wealth also frequently select this form of organization. A donor advised fund permits many unrelated donors to use the same core organization for the administration and investment of the philanthropic portion of their financial assets while permitting each donor to determine the philanthropic purposes to which her or his individual fund will be dedicated. The sharing of costs that a donor advised fund affords permits each family in the fund to do more with its philanthropic dollars than it could if it had to support the full costs of its own individual organization. A donor advised fund makes it possible for every family in America to increase the strength of its family balance sheet by sharing the values of giving and learning that flow from philanthropy.

Regardless of the type of philanthropy a family selects, the decision to organize the family to do its philanthropic work together contains within it the same issues of governance as arise in all other joint family decisions. A philanthropy must be as carefully organized as every other entity within the family governance structure if it is to carry out, with excellence, its special role in wealth preservation and if it is to be integrated properly into the family's overall structure.

Many families use the organization of a philanthropic entity as the first step in the construction of their wealth-preservation structures, recognizing that it offers the family a mechanism for learning together about the following issues:

I. Objective business issues
    A. Different forms of legal entities and the purposes for which each is used
    B. The investment of assets
        1. Modern portfolio theory
        2. Asset allocation
    C. The administration of assets
    D. Taxation

E. The supervisory role of the courts and other governmental organizations

F. Accounting

G. The role of management in an organization

H. The role of a board of directors in an organization
   1. Classes of directors
      a. Family members
      b. Outside directors
   2. Terms of directors

I. The role of the shareholders in an organization

J. Distribution of assets through grant making

K. Peer review (see Chapter 14)

II. Subjective business issues

L. Each family member's passion expressed through his or her grant making

M. Each family member's values in the creation of a mission statement for the family's philanthropic goals

N. The values the family wishes to express to others

O. Learning about other people and their values through grant making

P. Holding people within and outside of the family accountable for how they carry out their assigned tasks

Q. The extraordinary fun of being together and learning together

R. The strengths and weaknesses of each family member and how to enhance the strengths and buffer the weaknesses

S. The experience of making mistakes together and why every great organization wants its members to make mistakes: because we all learn more from our mistakes than from our successes

T. The ability to forgive each other

U. How to be a leader and how to choose one

V. How to be a representative and how to choose representatives

W. How to hold a meeting

As you will appreciate by now, the organization and operation of a philanthropic entity is a microcosm of all the issues present in the organization and operation of every entity on the family balance sheet. The positive family dynamic of starting a long-term wealth preservation plan with a philanthropic organization uses the family's desire to help others as its first forum for learning to work together. Starting with philanthropy does not reduce the complex and difficult emotions each family member faces in any discussions on becoming a partner in a joint family undertaking. Each family member will have to determine her or his willingness to invest a part of her or his human, intellectual, and financial capital in such a joint enterprise. When difficult issues arise in the formation of a family philanthropy, and they will, they must be acknowledged as family risks of doing business together, just as in the organization of every other joint family enterprise.

I am a great believer in starting hard work, especially work that requires an individual to give up some freedom for a larger group goal, with small steps that are likely to be successful. If a family is organizing itself for long-term wealth preservation, all kinds of individual issues will arise as each individual decides whether to be a member of the family for this purpose. Philanthropy offers family members a chance to "test the water" of family business membership through the pooling of some part of their philanthropic activities, rather than plunging into what may turn out to be a very cold bath by contributing all of their individual financial assets to the long-term family wealth preservation business only.

Philanthropy is an extremely important part of every family governance system. It offers every family the chance to experience the joy of rediscovering its most important values and offers a family a way to share the thrill of successfully helping others. Most important, it tightens family bonds—the family glue—by recognizing and acknowledging the creativity and passions of each member.

Successful philanthropy creates new family stories of family heroes and heroines. These are the stories that will teach later generations that family wealth preservation lies in the successful pursuit of happiness of each individual family member.[1]

Chapter Notes

1. For readers who are interested in the story of how a family used philanthropy as a step in creating family, I strongly recommend a book titled *Building Family Unity Through Giving: The Story of the Namaste Foundation,* by Deanne Stone, self-published by The Whitman Institute, 1992.

Chapter Thirteen

Evaluating the
Next Generation

W HEN A FAMILY decides to work against the tendencies
described by the shirtsleeves proverb, they need tools with
which to gauge the success of their development. This evaluation is
most important in the next generation, because they will become
the new family governors. Some criteria must be established to
assess the capability of the next generation to carry on.[1]

To begin the process, I suggest that the family and its evaluators look back at its earlier generations to see where the family has
been and to know where it is now, so it can know where it is going.
The shirtsleeve proverb is helpful here, since it suggests that the
family look at the current and just-previous generations to measure the next generation's position against the proverb's predicted
pattern. Let's not forget, in making this review, that each current
member of a family is simultaneously a first-generation member
of his or her nuclear family, a second-generation member of two
families, and a third-generation member of four families. If we
are to make this review complete, we need to review all of these
families' histories. I suggest such a survey apply the same evaluation criteria, described below, to the current and just-previous
generations as to the next generation. Finally, as a family begins
an evaluation process, it should describe to all of its members the
risk of which the proverb speaks. Members should know why the

family is compiling this information so that, hopefully, all family members will agree to the process.

It is important that the evaluators representing the first and second generations seek by this process to express four things to the members of the third generation:

- **First,** the first and second generations' love for them;
- **Second,** the first and second generations' desire for them to live lives in which they pursue personal journeys of happiness;
- **Third,** the first and second generation's desire to work with them to *enhance* their individual pursuits of happiness; and
- **Fourth,** the gratitude of the second generation to the first for their own lives of individual happiness, as a model for gratitude in its deepest dimension.

It is my view that these expressions provide to an entire family an in-depth answer to why a family might undertake a process of evaluation. They imply that a family engaging in such a process desires to inform itself on how to enhance the individual lives of its members in pursuit of the dynamic preservation of the family as a whole.

Before moving to the criteria on which the evaluation process will be based, on what criteria will it *not* be based? First, it will not evaluate the success of the third generation based on whether its members are dreaming the dreams of their second-generation parents. Second, it will not offer stories of how the second generation dreamed the dreams of the first generation. Why not? Because no member of our species has ever been able to dream another's dreams. It is my observation that families who base their criteria for success on this principle fall to the proverb every time.

On what question, then, should the evaluation be based? I suggest that the second generation, through the evaluators, ask each member of the third, What is your dream? And how can I invest in it?

Let me hasten here to make it clear that I'm not talking about a financial investment. I'm talking about the second generation (and the first, if it is living) investing its human and intellectual capital in the dreams of the third. Such investment may at a later stage call for financial capital, but in my experience, it's the second and first generations' willingness to put their human and intellectual skins in the third generation's game that matters. What further intuition to a successful family future lies beneath this question of the third generation's dreams? I suggest that it is found in two ideas that lie at the root of Western philosophy: Socrates' suggestion that our individual work in this life is to "Know thyself," and Aristotle's suggestion that our central pursuit be that of seeking individual happiness. In seeking to know ourselves I believe each of us begins the critical journey to self-awareness and, hopefully, to happiness in its deepest sense. Perhaps, if we are successful, we will become elders and mentors to the next generations of our families.

What questions should the evaluators ask to determine whether family members are seeking to know themselves and pursuing happiness in their life journeys? Among them might be the following:

1) Is the person I am evaluating free, or is he or she dependent?

2) Is this person self-aware?

3) Has this person sought to know his or her calling? If yes, is he or she pursuing it? If not, why not?

4) Does this person perceive the difference in work as calling and work as wages?

5) Has this person had a mentor in pursuing this calling? Does he or she have a mentor now in pursuing his or her calling, or in any other area of his or her life? If not, does he or she have the skills to find one?

6) Has this person the humility to be an apprentice in order not only to learn the body of knowledge required to pursue his or her calling but to undertake the process of learning itself? Has this person been an apprentice? Has this person mastered something so he or she understands, and has lived out, the process of learning that comes with passing through the stages of apprenticeship to journeyman to master?

7) Does this person understand the difference between hubris and humility and the consequences to his or her pursuit of happiness of each of them?

8) Does this person have friends? Who is he or she to such friends?

9) Can this person express love?

10) Can this person express compassion for himself or herself and for others?

11) Can this person express gratitude?

12) Can this person express joy and humor?

13) Does this person have a view of what is true, what is good, what is beautiful, and what is just or right?

14) Can this person balance justice with mercy?

15) Does this person perceive the difference between courage and bullying?

16) Does this person take active roles in the larger civil society? In stewarding and giving to others?

17) In which of the areas previously mentioned is this person competent, and in which areas is growth required?

It is in these questions that the evaluator will discover the essence of each member of the third generation. As the evaluator comes to an appreciation of each third-generation member, he or she will begin to perceive the state of the third generation's human and intellectual capital. The evaluator will also be enabled to develop a plan of action for the lifelong learning of each third-generation member, so that each will be able to answer that yes, he or she is attempting to know him or herself, and yes, he or she is on a journey in pursuit of his or her personal happiness. With appropriate annual assessments, a family using such an evaluation process will have an enhanced possibility of preserving the family as a whole as it enhances the growth of its individual members' human and intellectual capital.

You have undoubtedly noted by now that other than as a passing reference, I have not mentioned evaluating the third generation's ability to deal with financial capital. I have done this purposefully because I believe that financial capital is the least important of the three capitals to an individual's successful pursuit of happiness. First, successful management of financial capital, in and of itself, cannot protect a family from fulfilling the prophecy of the shirtsleeves proverb. Financial capital is simply a material representation of goods and services; unlike human and intellectual capital, it has no intrinsic worth. Financial capital, at best, can only be a tool to grow a person's human and intellectual capital. Alone, it can't cultivate a human being or preserve a family. Second, families (especially those members who are called to financial careers) have told me that dealing with the human questions was too difficult, and like ostriches with their heads in the sand, they saw teaching financial competency as their only task. Again the proverb prevails.

Assuming that a family properly perceives the relative impact on its own success of financial competence, vis-à-vis human and intellectual competence, what then is an appropriate process for a family to use in understanding and evaluating its third-generation members' financial competence? Certainly, if third-generation family members have parents with wealth, they must achieve a level of financial competence or risk becoming dependent and losing their freedom. Perhaps this reality is at the root of the question often asked by newly wealthy parents of the New Economy as they consider their children and estate planning: How much is enough? A question that on its face appears quantitative, but that I believe is actually the qualitative question How do I, as a parent, avoid having trust-funder, or remittance-addicted, children? A third-generation child has a duty to himself or herself to achieve a reasonable level of financial competence. What level of competence? I suggest a level commensurate with the statistical reality that in the DNA shuffle of our parents' genes that brings us into being, the likelihood that we are called to financial careers is minute. Therefore, I suggest it ought to be a level of competence equivalent to the Princeton University course Physics 101 for Poets, which required poets to become competent in the principles of physics but was not a stepping-stone to a career in the field.

Given these realities, how can an evaluator assess the financial competence of third-generation family members?

I suggest that the evaluator start by considering to what degree financial capital seems integral to each such individual's calling (as determined by the questions above). For instance, if a member of the third generation becomes a priest and takes a vow of poverty, where does financial competence fit? Suppose another family member is a master sculptor, for whom $20,000 in annual income provides her with $5,000 to give away? Of course, these are extreme examples used to pry open our minds to the reality that many of the persons the evaluator will review are deeply engaged in human, intellectual, and spiritual pursuits in which financial capital plays a very small part. What criteria, then, might an evaluator apply in assessing the financial competency of third-generation members?

- **First,** does he or she have an excellent process for evaluating possible advisers in all fields, not just financial? How well is he or she choosing mentors and using them?
- **Second,** does he or she understand the double helix of the interweaving of risk and reward?
- **Third,** does he or she understand the twin concepts of stewardship of generational financial wealth and dynamic preservation of financial capital?
- **Fourth,** does he or she feel and accept the reciprocal obligation to the family and its financial capital that grows out of the first-, second-, and other third-generation family members' investments of their human and intellectual capital in his or her individual pursuit of happiness? Does he or she actively work to instill financial knowledge in the next generation of the family?
- **Fifth,** does he or she participate in family governance by undertaking the lifelong learning that a family engaged in dynamic preservation offers him or her?
- **Sixth,** does he or she actively seek competence, and eventually excellence, in managing financial relationships as a beneficiary, as a limited partner, as a shareholder, as an owner, as a member of various family boards both for profit and not for profit, or in any other financial relationships within the family?

While this list is not exhaustive and each evaluator will add or subtract as the individual circumstances of the evaluated dictate, it is a start, I hope, in developing questions that will answer the desires of earlier-generation members that there be financial competence, while recognizing what appropriate levels of competence are for individuals who are not called to financial careers.

I'm sure some readers will ask why I have not mentioned the evaluation of third-generation members' social capital, nor have I offered criteria for measuring the role of social capital in their lives. I have done this purposefully. In my opinion, the amount of social capital a family has is a function of how well each family member knows him or herself and how he or she expresses that knowledge in dealings with the larger world. Philanthropy—giving and stewardship, the means by which we express our love for our fellow humans—is an expression of who we are. Social capital, therefore, is, in my opinion, the *result* of a family's intentional enhancement of the human and intellectual capital of its members. Social capital is important, but it can be evaluated by measuring the next generation's human and intellectual capital and need not be assessed separately. Whether a family's social capital is growing or shrinking is a reflection of whether its human and intellectual capital is thriving. Thus to whatever extent those two capitals are expanding or diminishing, families will or will not enhance the lives of others and the communities of which they are parts

I hope I have convinced you that the state of an individual's human and intellectual capital is the critical issue to evaluate in determining how well he or she, or the family of which he or she is a part, will do in eluding the prediction of the shirtsleeves proverb. I also hope that the questions I have offered will help evaluators to successfully assess these two critical components of a family's wealth, both to aid in the growth of these capitals and, even more important, to enable the earlier generations of a family to contribute to each third-generation family member's individual pursuit of happiness.

In my work with families, I have learned that *assessment, measurement,* and *evaluation* are words that frequently bring fear to people whose learning styles did not make school a happy place,[2] or to those whose parents or grandparents asked them to dream their dreams. I have also learned that when employed by a family unmindfully or without comprehending the true diversity of the multiple callings of its members, an assessment or evaluation can *depreciate* a family's human and intellectual capital—a family's most precious resources. An evaluation is an especially frightening process when the results determine whether one will or will not receive that portion of a family's financial capital necessary to pursue one's dreams.

In my opinion, every family attempting to grow and dynamically preserve itself needs family members whose dreams are creative and filled with curiosity and who, through the living out of those dreams, become free and independent persons. In my experience, families of this type welcome mistakes for the learning they encourage, while always ensuring that their most valuable assets—their young— do not come to harm. Families do not need family members who are fearful or dependent because they have been asked to dream others' dreams or exhorted to be perfect, making no mistakes from which a lesson might emerge.

Chapter Notes

1. This chapter is in part excerpted and adapted from a paper that was first delivered at The Next Generation Colloquium sponsored by Citibank on December 6, 2000.

2. For a discussion of learning styles, please see *Frames of Mind: The Theory of Multiple Intelligences,* by Howard Gardner (Basic Books, 1993) and *Emotional Intelligence: Why It Can Matter More Than IQ,* by Daniel P. Goleman (Bantam Books, 1995).

Chapter Fourteen

Peer Review

WHEN AN INDIVIDUAL creates a long-term trust or charitable organization, he rarely considers that such an organism is subject to the same entropy or gradual decay and eventual depletion of its energy as are all other living things. This reality is only discovered when later generations of beneficiaries find they are dealing with atrophied trustees or when the purposes of the charitable organization are no longer being fulfilled. Necessarily, the law provides remedies in cases of serious misfeasance and neglect, but the law offers no positive program to overcome or even to reduce the effects of entropy. I often wonder whether the grantors of long-term trusts and founders of perpetual charitable organizations would have permitted these organisms to have been born at all had they fully understood how unlikely it is that their desires would be fully met. After watching the action of entropy on trusts and charitable organizations, I decided to try to find a method of governance that might counteract or at least substantially retard its effect. To this end I studied various systems of governance used by family and nonprofit organizations to see if I could find a model that worked. My search ultimately led to the system of accreditation used by educational institutions called peer review.

In this process, an institution voluntarily submits all aspects of itself to a rigorous review by its peer organizations. In the academic context such a review can lead to a negative conclusion as drastic as loss of accreditation. Despite this risk, the review is generally seen as a positive process by institutions that would otherwise have little sense of how well they were doing. In studying great educational institutions, such as Princeton University, that have rigorously practiced peer review, whether in the microcosm of the granting of doctoral degrees or in the macrocosm of the institutions themselves, it is clear how successfully the process can be used to maintain excellence. When this process is applied to trusts and charitable organizations, it is used only as a positive process. The courts would handle any negative process. Peer review provides a trust or charitable organization with an opportunity for its peers to determine how well it is meeting its mission and how it might do so even more successfully. If executed properly, peer review is energizing in the extreme and, therefore, offers great hope that the process of entropy can be effectively retarded.

Assuming a family wished to include peer review in its governance, how would that work in the context of a trust or charitable organization?

I. The instruments creating the trust or charitable organization should include a requirement for such periodic review. While there are many existing trusts and charitable organization whose instruments can not be modified to include provisions for peer review, families may still implement the process by requiring existing trustees to voluntarily agree to be peer reviewed. In the case of successor trustees who undertake their duties following implementation of peer review, such trustees can be required to accept the principle of peer review as a condition of their qualification as trustees.

II. All trustees should reaffirm their understanding of the process and their commitment to its successful conclusion before beginning a peer review.

III. The selection of peer reviewers should be undertaken by an individual or organization designated to carry out this function in the trust agreement or charitable organization documents, or by a committee of selectors chosen by such an individual or organization. Persons selected to be peer reviewers should have no close relationship to the entity under review or to any trustee or director associated with it. The reviewers should also have no close association with any beneficiary of any trust being reviewed or with any organization funded by any charitable organization. Preferably the reviewers should be individuals or organizations of proven excellence in the trust or charitable areas and with long experience in the field. Peer reviewers should serve only once in this capacity in order to ensure that each review stands on its own and in order to minimize the possibility of contamination of the process by politicization.

IV. Peer reviewers should be compensated in order to assure that they apply the same degree of rigor to the process as they do to their other professional endeavors. The selector should be responsible for negotiating the reviewers' compensation.

V. A peer review should occur every five years, although some families are considering reviews every three years.

VI. The peer review should cover all aspects of the trust or charitable organization.

A. In the case of a trust, the reviewers should consider the following issues and such others as are specific to that case:

1. The grantor's original purpose in creating the trust, the trustee's awareness of the purposes of the trust, and whether these purposes are guiding the trustee.

2. The trustee's relations with the beneficiaries in general and, specifically, whether the trust's actual operation is empowering to the beneficiaries.

3. The trustee's awareness of the beneficiaries' situations and the trustee's success in enhancing their situations within the provisions of the trust.

4. The level of financial awareness of the beneficiaries and what mechanisms are in place to continually improve their financial capabilities.

5. The trustee's awareness of each beneficiary's choice of life journey and what mechanisms are in place to continually enhance pursuit of each such beneficiary's goals.

6. The trustee's general policies and procedures and the implementation of them as they relate to the following:
   a. The trust's investment goals and its success in meeting them
   b. The selection and provision of investment advice and management
   c. The trust's tax position
   d. The selection of tax services
   e. The trust's legal position
   f. The selection of legal services

B. In the case of a charitable organization, the reviewers should consider the following:
   1. The director's awareness of the mission of the organization, the founder's original purpose in creating it, and whether those purposes are still guiding the organization.
   2. If the original mission has been completed, is there a new mission? If so, how was the new mission determined, and is it clear that all directors understand the new mission and actively advocate it?
   3. If there is a new mission, are the current directors and executives fully trained and knowledgeable in the new field? Are other persons better able to achieve the new mission?
   4. If the organization was set up as an operating foundation, is the entity it is operating thriving?
   5. If the organization was set up as a grant-making foundation, do its policies and procedures carry out its function properly?
   6. The organization's general policies and procedures as they relate to the following:
      a. The organization's investment goals and its success in meeting them
      b. The selection and provision of investment advice and management
      c. The organization's tax position
      d. The selection of tax services

      e. The organization's legal position

      f. The selection of legal services

VII. The peer reviewers should have access to all documents, reports, accounts, tax returns, professionals retained by the entity, beneficiaries, grant recipients, and other information necessary to properly carry out their review and to determine whether the recommendations of any prior review were implemented. In the process, the peer reviewers will interview the trustees, beneficiaries, and professionals involved with the trust and the directors, officers, professionals, and principal grant recipients (where appropriate) involved with the charitable organization.

VIII. The peer review should last one day and should be wholly constructive, since its purpose is to create a positive basis for the trust's or charitable organization's ongoing operations. The review should offer a clear picture of the current status of the trust or charitable organization. It should raise important issues, problems, and questions on how the trust or charitable organization might better meet its mission. The peer review should not focus on the negative. In fact, should the peer review discover any serious deficiencies, the review should be aborted and the problem issues brought to the attention of the peer review selector for proper correction. While termination of the peer review may seem a drastic result, once the positive atmosphere of the review has been reduced, the full positive affects of the review can no longer be achieved. The peer review should not attempt to solve problems or answer important questions raised by the review; solutions and answers are the province of the trustees or directors, and not of the peer reviewers. The difference between the reviewer who raises issues and the implementer who resolves the issues is a critical component of the process and must be recognized as vital to its success. The peer reviewers are not the trustees or the directors and must not enter into the discretionary realms that the latter properly exercise.

IX. Sole responsibility for implementation of the peer review's suggestions must be with the trustees or directors.

X. Peer reviewers should have no responsibility to assess whether any of the review's suggestions are implemented, although it may be appropriate in a specific instance and without further compensation for further inquiry to be made of a peer reviewer on the details of a specific issue raised during the review.

XI. Implementation of suggestions arising out of the peer review process should *not* be assigned to any individual or organization that served as a reviewer during the peer review which initiated the suggestion. It is imperative that no possible professional self-interest on the part of any peer reviewer enters into the process.

Chapter Fifteen

The Private Trust Company

This chapter is dedicated to Sara Hamilton, the founder of the Family Office Exchange, a great friend, a pioneer, and my closest companion on the path to learning how to help families preserve their wealth.

I DEBATED WHETHER to include this chapter in the book since it deals with a subject of limited application. The costs of chartering and operating a private trust company make it prohibitively expensive for families with less than $60 million. However, private trust companies have proven to be such a powerful tool in long-term family governance for the families who have created them that I decided the book would be incomplete without a discussion of the idea. For the vast majority of readers whose families will not charter a private trust company, this chapter offers a reprise of many of the ideas on family governance set out in other parts of the book.

The term private trust company (PTC) was coined to describe a corporation that is formed to provide fiduciary services to a single family, as opposed to a corporation that offers its service to everyone. Many state laws refer to such an entity as a limited-purpose trust company. In the balance of this chapter, I will use the term PTC to cover both a trust company that voluntarily limits its services to one family and a limited-purpose trust company.

In order for a PTC to accept fiduciary assignments, it must obtain a charter from one of the fifty-one state banking commissions or from the Office of the Controller of the Currency of the United States. Among the requirements for obtaining such a charter are (1) the investment of substantial capital in the PTC—

the specific limits are set by the chartering body; and (2) proof to the chartering body that the board of directors and management of the proposed PTC have the necessary experience to properly operate a trust company. The PTC must agree to be regulated on an ongoing basis by the chartering body and to follow a variety of very detailed policies and procedures. Once a PTC is formed and operating, it is entitled to offer to the members of the family who chartered it all types of fiduciary services.

The history of PTCs in the United States often helps families understand how a PTC might fit into their family governance structures. The oldest PTC I'm aware of that is still functioning today is United States Trust Company (USTCo). USTCo was set up in the 1850s by four families to provide fiduciary services to their families. Some years later USTCo evolved to provide fiduciary services to outside families, and it then moved from being a PTC to the corporate trustee we know today. At the turn of the century the Phipps family and the Smith family evolved what have come down to us as Bessemer Trust Company and Northern Trust Company respectively. Again, they each created a PTC to provide services to their families, and those PTCs later evolved to provide services to others. These families saw a need for a long-term trustee to provide part of a system of family governance.

Between the 1920s and the 1970s few, if any, PTC charters appear to have been issued. I believe this apparent decline in the number of PTCs resulted not from families losing interest in the benefits of a PTC, but rather from state restrictions on granting charters. Most states, before they will issue a new trust company charter, require that there be a clearly demonstrated public demand for trust services that cannot be served by existing trust companies. Since most states have many existing trust companies, this "public need" test normally cannot be overcome.

In the 1970s and 1980s, however, a number of families were able to overcome the concerns of the legislators. Among these families were the Rockefellers, the Houghtons, the Pitcairns, the Cargill-MacMillans, the Cullens, and the Whittiers. In the 1990s—following the same path as USTCo, Bessemer, and Northern Trust—some of these family trust companies decided to offer their services to non-family clients and moved from PTC to corporate trustee status. In such cases these former PTCs have set very high minimum account sizes to ensure that families joining them will be able to use the handmade services they provide without a change in the character of their organizations. Most of the other PTCs mentioned here have chosen to continue providing their services exclusively to the members of the family that founded them.

The number of new PTCs seeking charters is currently mushrooming. There are multiple PTC applications pending in Wyoming, South Dakota, Nevada, Alaska, and Delaware. It is not surprising that these states have been chosen by families for their charter applications. Each of these states is pro-business; has no state income tax on trusts created by individuals who were not domiciled there when the trust was created; has up-to-date trust legislation; has shown a willingness to accommodate new ideas such as eliminating the Rule against Perpetuities; and, most important, has indicated an interest in the chartering of new PTCs. I think of these states as "islands" that, like Bermuda, Cayman, Hong Kong, and Singapore, are competing to become financial service centers to families of privilege.

What kind of atmosphere will a family considering forming a PTC encounter in the future? As the U.S. "islands" mentioned above compete for PTC business, I anticipate gradually falling initial capital requirements; special regulatory rules to accommodate the issues of a trust company that does not offer its services to the public; a regulatory environment that recognizes a family's right to confidentiality; and new trust legislation to accommodate the most advanced legal thinking on trustee best practices. Obviously, this competition offers an even more user-friendly atmosphere for the chartering of new PTCs.

Why would a family want to create a PTC? Families of significant wealth have the financial capacity to make or buy any service. When such a family decides to set up trusts or to change the trustees of existing trusts and considers the question of obtaining the highest quality trust services, it is natural to consider the option of creating its own trust company. In deciding what form of trustee will best accomplish the family's goals for trustee excellence, multiple objective issues must be assessed, including: (i) rate of turnover of personnel of corporate trustees, (ii) confidentiality, (iii) trustworthiness, (iv) financial status, (v) investment competence, (vi) location in a state without a state income tax, (vii) costs of director and officer insurance and fiduciary bonding, (viii) need for successors in the case of individuals, (ix) costs of chartering a PTC and of its ongoing operations, (x) trustees' commissions for outside individual or corporate trustees, and (xi) the subjective cost of in-house personnel management versus the cost of managing an outside relationship.

In addition to the objective assessment of which form of trustee will serve the family best, the family also must undertake a subjective assessment of its intentions regarding family governance and whether a PTC fits into its governance system for long-term wealth preservation.

What are the advantages of a PTC in a system of family governance?

1) The PTC is the administrative center of family business, the "family seat." It creates a place for governance of all kinds to take place, and a place for family members to meet and discuss long-term wealth preservation. The need for a family center as the family moves into the third, fourth, and fifth generations will be readily apparent.

2) The PTC will be managed to express the family's values in accordance with the family mission statement.

3) The PTC will be a repository for the family history.

4) The PTC will often merge with an existing family office to concentrate all services under its umbrella.

5) The PTC has a perpetual life, thus providing a significant improvement in solving trustee succession problems.

6) The family members elect the board of the PTC using selection criteria calling for excellence. The initial PTC board will be composed of family leaders and trusted outsiders.

7) The PTC board can evolve to meet the growth of family branches and the need for representation of all family power centers.

8) As the family evolves, PTC governance can be modified to reflect changes needed to meet new issues created by that evolution.

9) Family members will see PTC board members as representatives since they both elect them and can choose whether or not to re-elect them.

10) The PTC board is governed by the "business judgment rule" in making decisions. This standard of care permits individual PTC board members to make bolder investment decisions on the investment of individual trusts than they could if they were trustees of those individual trusts, where they would be governed by the "prudent man" or "prudent investor" rules. Families practicing investor allocation have found this PTC advantage particularly helpful.

11) The liability of PTC board members is limited to the capital of the PTC, assuming they have not acted recklessly or criminally. Individual trustees have no limitation on personal liability unless the particular trust agreement under which they are acting limits their liability.

12) PTCs have the right to create common trust funds to permit the pooling of individual accounts. This authority permits every family member, regardless of the size of his or her individual wealth, to participate in all investment sectors of the family asset allocation plan. It also greatly enhances possibilities for investor allocation. Common trust funds are not subject to SEC regulation, thus saving the hard costs of fees and the soft costs of time spent complying with regulations covering Registered Investment Advisors.

13) PTCs can be chartered in states with no state income tax.

14) PTCs will adopt affirmative trustee resignation policies, will instruct family members to provide in their trust agreements for a trustee's removal, and will advocate the use of protectors as alternative trustee/beneficiary dispute resolution mechanisms.

What are the disadvantages of a PTC in a system of family governance?

1) Increased hard costs. Outside corporate trustees offer economies of scale a PTC normally can't equal. PTCs bring new costs for additional or extended family meetings, for new skilled personnel, for outside advisers, and for bank regulation.

2) Increased soft costs. New family employees mean increased time burdens on family leaders to manage these people to achieve excellence. PTCs require meetings, elections, and so on. Each of these is an increased burden on family members' time.

3) Loss of confidentiality. While it is difficult to assess how serious this problem is, certainly PTC regulation by the appropriate banking authority will lead to the exchange with that authority of family information. While the regulatory process is confidential, leaks will always be a concern. There also is the risk with employee turnover that important family information will leave with the employee. Confidentiality agreements are the norm for all employees of PTCs.

4) Regulation by the appropriate banking authority means complying with an array of policies and procedures that change frequently. Compliance brings with it hard and soft costs.

5) Concerns of beneficiaries that the PTC will be colder and less friendly than individual trustees when discretionary distributions are under consideration. Protectors can help in these instances.

6) Concerns of family members that the PTC will begin with excellence but over time will fall into entropy due to a failure of family governance or commitment.

7) PTC administrative services may not be of the highest quality.

When a family has completed its assessment of the advantages and disadvantages of a PTC, it is going to find it difficult to reject the PTC option out of hand. The PTC clearly offers a family of substantial wealth the possibility of excellent user-friendly services at slightly higher costs. More important, a PTC can become a family seat, or center to which family members can look for leadership and services in their individual pursuits of wealth preservation. In this function a PTC offers a communications network through which the family's human and intellectual capitals can be collected and disseminated. Most importantly, a PTC offers a family a structure within which to create a long-term system of representative government through which the family can respond creatively to an ever-changing environment. A PTC practicing excellence offers its customers the highest level of administrative services, the boldest and most creative investment services, and Solomonic wisdom in its discretionary distribution discussions. It epitomizes "control without ownership."[1]

Chapter Notes

1. For readers who are interested in exploring the PTC in greater detail, the Family Office Exchange (www.foxexchange.com) has produced an excellent set of materials.

PART FOUR

Reflections

Chapter Sixteen

The Role of Aunts and Uncles

I HAVE OBSERVED that aunts and uncles are critically important to the development of their nieces and nephews into successful family members. Moreover, it is vital to a family's success that the formative roles played by aunts and uncles be acknowledged and supported.

Anthropology reveals that in tribal societies, when a boy or girl is passing through puberty and entering adulthood, often the boy's uncles and the girl's aunts take custody of their repective nephews and nieces to prepare them for their adult roles. These societies, as well as our modern ones, recognize that normal, healthy conflicts exist between parents and children as the children move toward individualization, adulthood, and independence. These conflicts make it unlikely that parents alone can effectively prepare their children to fulfill their adult roles in society. Tribal society intuits that the blood relationships we have with our aunts and uncles—after all, they share equally the original source of our parents' DNA—confer a strong bond that will permit them to successfully mentor us. To take this idea a step further, some biologists and psychologists believe that the impulse and set of behaviors we call altruism is almost as strong between aunts and uncles and their nephews and nieces as between parents and children, because they share a substantial part of one another's gene pools. With this strong biological connection and its assorted psychological realities, it is not surprising that aunts and uncles can be successful mentors to their nieces and nephews.

Looking at the process by which nieces and nephews become adult members of a tribe, we encounter the role of ritual in effecting successful passages from childhood to adulthood. Such rites of passage communicate to the girl or boy the importance of this transformation and ensure that as adults they will be fully ready to assume their duties and responsibilities in tribal life and governance. For the reasons explored above, their mentors through this critical passage to successful adulthood are frequently their aunts and uncles.

In our modern times, it is my experience that rarely are these important changes in the lives of boys and girls recognized as other than purely physical events. To be sure, the women of a family usually give certain advice and some ritual and ceremony to girls as they grow into women. Perhaps it is because women's ways of knowing and teaching serve the female development process better. Girls do seem to become women in the full psychological sense of adulthood more easily and more rapidly than boys become men. What I do know from my own practice, however, and anecdotally from many colleagues, is that I and they have many forty- and fifty-year-old boys as clients. I assure you I am not being jocular about this subject, dismissing it as an amusing quirk, as society does in saying that all men are really little boys inside. Unfortunately, it is my direct experience that our society is producing many males who never become men except in the biological sense.

What, you may ask, is my definition of a man? It is quite simply an adult male who is absolutely prepared to accept accountability for his actions, who is ready to say "I am responsible for my actions no matter what." He is a person who does not blame others for his choices and who does not play the victim. Why, you may ask, should our society, with all we know about the process of human development and its many phases, be failing to produce men and instead be producing eternal boys? I believe much of this problem grows out of our modern society's lack of ritual and even more from the disappearance of the critical roles in maturation that uncles traditionally played.

There is evidence for this view in some of the initiation rituals older societies created. In some cultures, a boy's first ritual kill as a hunter served this process, as did required vision quests. There were also periods of formal segregation from the tribe while being schooled in adult roles and responsibilities by uncles and their equivalents. In certain tribal societies, the boys were buried overnight. The boy's re-entrance and rebirthing the next morning as a man with a new name was an outward sign of his passage to adulthood. In our society, military service, going off to college, sporting activities, and particularly men-only activities under the direction of uncles used to serve a similar purpose. Today, most boys experience none of these events in the way they used to. Going to college and participating in sports are seen not as important rituals meant to carry a boy through the passage to adulthood but rather as opportunities for light play and heavy self-gratification. Even more rarely are such events supervised or conducted by uncles or their equivalents for the purpose of assisting boys through the rights of passage to manhood.

The problem with this trend in our social evolution is that life without ritual does not suit our species. Specifically, it leaves individual members of society without the experiences and tools necessary to understand the process of becoming an adult. I believe many individuals, and boys in particular, would be assisted in moving into adulthood if our society offered, through updated rituals, the exclamation points we need to define the critical passages in the journey.

Johan Huizinga, a noted Dutch historian and philosopher, wrote a book called *Homo Ludens: A Study of the Play-Element in Culture* (Beacon Press, 1971). Huizinga's thesis is that the characteristic that most distinguishes our species from all others is our capacity for creative play. Through play, and the consequences of it, we learn and mature. Huizinga's view of play encompasses all activities that engage our curiosity and creativity, activities central, he believes, to how and why we as a species thrive. In many families in earlier times, including mine, some of the best moments of play came with aunts and uncles. I believe I learned more about life in moments of play with my aunts Dorothy, Dorothea, and Margretha than at most other times. Certainly the rewards—the lessons both positive and negative—that I received from these moments remain strongly in my memory. Perhaps it is these special experiences that piqued my curiosity and led to this reflection.

I would be delighted if I could now list the two or three rituals assisted by aunts and uncles that would guarantee all boys and girls a successful passage from childhood to adulthood. As both a caring parent and grandparent and a helping professional, I only wish I knew. Perhaps if girls seem to be achieving greater success in this regard than boys, it will be through studying their process that answers will emerge. I do believe that if aunts and uncles resume their traditional roles, using modern rituals based on Huizinga's remarkable insight on the role of play in our species' success, good results will appear. At a time in our species' history when we must face the extraordinary new questions posed by our exploding global population, we need all members of *Homo sapiens* to pass successfully to adulthood in order for our species to assume its responsibilities to our planet. These are responsibilities that only initiated adults can undertake.

Whether or not you agree with any of these ideas, I hope you will reacquaint yourself with the significant roles aunts and uncles play in the critical passages of our journeys from childhood to adulthood. I particularly hope you will consider the situation of boys and young men in our society, and in your own way help them to become men. Our society has done extraordinary things in the last thirty years for women, although it has a great deal farther to go. Now let's see if we can do a similar service for men and in the process offer to all members of the human family the opportunity to become individuals capable of the lifelong learning that only mature adults enjoy.

Meanwhile, thanks to each of you who is an aunt or uncle for the rituals you perform, and will perform, in helping your nephews and nieces become adults.

Chapter Seventeen

The Art and Practice
of Mentorship

This chapter is dedicated to John O'Neil, with thanks for the many profound questions he has put to me and to so many others.

M ENTOR APPEARS FOR the first time in the western canon as a character in *The Odyssey*.[1] We are told by Homer that Mentor is an old and deeply respected man into whose hands Odysseus has given the kingdom of Ithaca while Odysseus sails away to fight the war with Troy. We are also told that Mentor has the duty of bringing up Telemachus, Odysseus' son, so that should Odysseus not return from the war, Telemachus can eventually become the king in Odysseus' stead. Mentor thus represents two roles: first, that of regent, a person of deep trustworthiness who can safely hold the space for another, while that other goes on a quest; second, that of the elder and teacher who can instill knowledge in another, particularly wisdom about the other person's journey of self-discovery. No sooner does Mentor take on these roles than Homer has Athena, the goddess of wisdom, take over the shell of Mentor's body and, masquerading as Mentor, give advice and assistance to Telemachus in his journey of personal growth. Then, at the end of the first part of *The Odyssey*, Mentor, inhabited by Athena, appears as a peacemaker, giving critical advice to all parties on how they may end their war and attain the riches of peace. Here is yet a third role of Mentor, as an elder person of wisdom assisting a whole country in its journey to achieve peace.

161

In these three roles we begin to see what the art of mentorship may be. I find it fascinating that Homer in Mentor combines the virtue of intelligence and the virtue of intuition in the same character. I find it even more fascinating that the interior and thus senior virtue of the masquerade is Mentor as intuition, as epitomized by Athena, goddess of wisdom, rather than Mentor as intelligence, as would be epitomized by Apollo or Zeus. I suggest you keep this metaphor in mind throughout this discussion, because my study and practice of mentorship confirms what Homer knew: that true mentorship is the expression by a mentor of wisdom through intuition in guiding another, a mentee, toward greater self-awareness and freedom in the mentee's journey in pursuit of happiness.[2]

What Mentorship Is Not

If one knows what true mentorship is, what then is it not? As was explained in Chapter 8, it is not teaching, or coaching, or being a best friend, or eldering. Each of these roles represents an important relationship, but none is that of a mentor. Why? Let's review each of these and see.

Teaching. In teaching, one person, the teacher, imparts data and information and sometimes knowledge to another person. The teacher does not expect to learn from the student, nor does the student expect to teach the teacher. In uncommon instances when the learning comes principally from the student's own questions and experiences, we approach the boundary between teaching and mentoring.

Coaching. A coach transmits specific skills to a trainee who wishes to acquire or enhance those skills. The greatest coaches will, before beginning to coach the trainee, seek to determine how the trainee learns. In Hindu practices for the development of a yogi,[3] the first effort of the guru to whom the aspirant turns to learn this art is to discover how the aspirant learns. The guru does this to determine whether he is the proper coach for this aspirant, and will refer the aspirant to another guru if appropriate. Great coaches know that they cannot coach every trainee, because their method of exchanging skills and practices cannot meet all learning styles. They, like the guru, know their own strengths and weaknesses. Lesser coaches take all comers, with a concomitant lessening of the possibility of learning by their trainees. Great coaches seek to know the trainee as a unique vessel for skill building, and insofar as they do, they approximate one of the arts of mentorship.

Being a best friend. Best-friend relationships are connections of the heart. Both parties believe that they can raise and discuss with the other their most intimate feelings and questions. In a mentoring relationship, it is only one party's questions—the mentee's—that form the basis of the dialogue. This is the sacred bond of the mentor and mentee. On the other hand, great friendships may develop out of mentorship relationships. Such friendships should be begun after the mentoring is completed so as not to confuse the boundaries of mentor and friend.

Eldering. All tribes grant to certain members—often elders—authority to be keepers of the tribe's stories and rituals, its sacred space. It is to them that the tribe looks when difficult decisions must be made about the roles and relationships of the members of the tribe. Today we look to certain people as elders because we perceive that they are wise. We believe that their wisdom about life will enhance our ability to mature well. We ask them to help us with the rituals of moving from childhood to adulthood, from the learning to the doing stage of life. We further ask them to help us with the rituals of moving from adulthood to elderhood, from the doing to the being stage of life. Relationships with elders improve our individual journeys toward happiness. Elders are like mentors in that they pose questions and teach us through story and metaphor. Unlike mentors, they are not proactive and have responsibilities that are community-wide rather than toward single individuals.

The Six Functions of a Mentor

Now that we understand what a mentor is and is not, what are a mentor's particular functions?

1) Mentoring is about asking questions, not about giving answers. A mentor's questions should guide us to the deepest possible learning about ourselves.

Great mentors seek to know us. We grant them the right to ask us the questions we least want to answer. With mentors we share our deepest passions and dreams when, to paraphrase Dante, "We find ourselves sitting in the middle of a dark wood with nowhere to go."[4] When we need a person who can help us form the questions that will lead us from a profoundly stuck, empty place like that described by Dante, we can all hope that *our* Virgils, Dante's Mentor, will appear and offer to lead us, but only if we are willing to descend to the depths of ourselves with our individual Virgils as our guides and interlocutors. Here is mentoring at its highest calling and in its most profound application. Being mentored, we learn *how* we learn and then design a process of learning unique to ourselves. Great mentors understand that their first duty is to ascertain how the aspirant or mentee learns, in order to determine whether they can in fact mentor this individual. No mentoring relationship can work without clarity on this point.

2) Successful mentoring is a dialogue in which both parties learn something essential. Unlike the other four forms of relationship discussed above, mentoring involves joint learning. I have not found this point often addressed. I do know that whenever I have been asked to mentor, I have learned much more than I imparted. The people by whom I have been lucky to have been mentored have made this same observation. Because mentoring occurs on many intuitional planes, it is not surprising that both parties at such a level of intimacy would deepen their individual self-awareness.

3) Mentoring requires both parties to commence their work together as apprentices in the Zen sense of having "beginner's minds."[5] We must be willing to admit at the most profound depths of our spirits that we don't know and that we are willing and ready to learn. To begin every session with our mentor with the wonder of the beginner is to give ourselves the greatest gift imaginable toward successful learning. Asking someone to mentor us and then starting every session "knowing it all," arguing at every turn or trying to be the master of the subject when we haven't left the apprentice place—these are the actions of a fool and simply make it clear that we are not ready to be mentored. For the mentor the beginner's mind is crucial to success. The mentor never knows at the beginning of each session where the mentee's questions will lead. The mentor can only know that by being open to the mentee's questions, the mentor may be able to deepen those questions and by doing so open new pathways for learning.

4) Mentorship employs any of three modes for this mutual learning:

> a. First, the path of Data→Information→Knowledge→ Wisdom
>
> b. Second the path of Seeking→Journeying→Listening→ Exchanging→Integrating
>
> c. Third, the path of Breaking Away/Differentiating→ Pausing/Listening/Learning→Integrating

Each of these paths offers the mentor and the mentee a process of successful learning. To me each says the same thing but with words that are sufficiently different that they resonate differently to the listener. Hopefully one of these paths will resonate so well that it will emerge as the mutual learning process to be used for a successful mentoring relationship. Deciding at the beginning of the mentoring relationship how the mentor and mentee can best learn together is just as important as discerning the mentee's individual style of learning.

5) Mentorship requires that both parties begin by agreeing on how it will end. I discuss this point at length later in the chapter. Here I will simply say that a mentoring relationship must have the cleanest and clearest possible boundaries. To paraphrase Robert Frost, high stone walls (boundaries) make good neighbors (mentors/mentees). While at the beginning of any good relationship we do consider boundaries, we rarely consider how such relationships should end. The mentor/mentee relationship presupposes that it begins because the mentee has questions that she or he perceives must be answered if her or his individual journey is to be successful.

Equally, the relationship assumes that when the mentee has found the answers within herself or himself, that the role will end. This last boundary is critical for both parties' success and well-being. New questions in the journey of the mentee will require new mentors. This is not to say that the former mentor is not the right person to continue the dialogue on these new issues. Rather, it is to both parties' benefits to recognize that the mentee must, in honoring the mentoring relationship properly, pause to consider who the best person is to help with her or his new questions. Honoring the relationship by ending it and opening a new search usually honors the relationship best. To do that well, the relationship must begin with a clear process for knowing how it will come to an end.

6) Finally, for a successful mentoring relationship, each party to it must be able to answer with an open heart and mind the following questions.

For the mentee when seeking a mentor: For the deepest questions I now have in my life, who will best be able to help me form these questions and help me in dialogue with myself to find those answers that will most enhance my self-awareness in my journey in pursuit of happiness?

For the mentor when asked to be a mentor: In what way can I enhance the self-awareness of this particular individual and thus enhance his or her journey in pursuit of happiness, and what will I learn about myself in doing so?

In my life, when seeking a mentor or when being asked to be one, these are the two questions that I have found open the greatest possibility for a successful mentoring relationship. I hope they will help you as they have helped me have successful mentoring relationships.

Willingness to be mentored is the greatest gift we can give ourselves. To be asked to be a mentor is the highest gift we can bestow upon another. To act as a mentor is the highest service any of us can render to another. To do this well is as complicated a process as human nature knows because of its intimacy and because it risks damage to another human being should it go awry. It is, therefore, a relationship of the highest order, based as it is in the giving of complete trust, one to another, with the nakedness and openness of spirit such a gift entails. Not to have a mentor is to risk finding oneself in a dark world with no place to go and without a Virgil's deep love to see us safely out.

Now that you understand the functions and importance of a mentor, how do you go about finding one?

The ancient Greeks had a saying, "When the student is ready, the teacher will appear." In my experience, the Greeks were absolutely right. I keep finding in my practice that in a seemingly magical way, when the about-to-be-student announces his or her readiness to learn, the teacher does appear. In addition I discern, deep in the statement of readiness, the humility of the person willing to become an apprentice to a master and, with it, the ability to honor another's wisdom. More and more I have come to realize that a critical virtue for a successful life is humility, the antithesis of hubris. Humility permits a human being to know what he or she does not know and to seek out others, whom we call teachers, who can provide answers to his or her questions. This process of seeking is at once ancient and absolutely modern. It is a ritual that must, in my opinion, precede any successful learning endeavor.

In Chapter 8, I discuss the initial steps an individual must take in seeking a mentor. The first is to determine what exactly, at this stage of his or her life, he or she is seeking to learn. This may be something external—a body of knowledge; or something internal—a deeper understanding of oneself.

Often we believe we are seeking something external when in fact we are really changing internally, and it is there we should begin. Many of the mystic traditions tell us that the intellect is the product of the intuition, that our minds are the reflections of our spirits. In my own life, I frequently find that when my intellect tells me I am at a crossroads and I must make a decision, I have in fact already answered the question through my intuition and am well down one of the paths, looking backward at the receding crossroad. Understanding what question we are really asking—is it exterior or interior? is it a question of intellect or of spirit?—is critical to knowing where to seek a mentor.

When the mentee has established the question for which he or she is seeking an answer, the next step is to begin to ask that question of the people we most trust. At this point the would-be mentee must have the courage to be vulnerable. The mentee must be willing to surrender his or her natural anxiety about asking others for help and the often-feared sense of owing that comes from asking someone for help. As long as the mentee is consciously resisting this act of surrender, he or she is not truly ready to learn, and the mentor will, in my experience, not appear. When the mentee has let go of this fear and opened him or herself up to the conscious commitment to another person that is necessary to be successfully mentored, the mentor will appear. Why should this be? Simply because those we trust the most, our inner circle, know when we are ready for our next learning. When we can convince them we are truly willing to begin that learning, they will help us find the mentor.

Often the members of the mentee's inner circle, at the beginning of the process, have no more idea of where to find the mentor than the mentee does. Working together, and using the multiple external relationships every group has, the mentor is almost always found. In today's world this is made easier by the information systems our society has at its command; imagine how much more difficult it was for people in small towns and villages before such systems existed. In discussing this step in the process of seeking a mentor, I am frequently challenged by individuals who state that they have no inner circle. Thus far, I have never found that to be true. In each case I have found that a few gentle questions lead to a list of helpful people; a list that seems to have been hidden from the mentee by his or her anxiety about asking for assistance. One cannot begin the journey of learning without asking for help. It is the crucial act for learning to occur.

The process does not end once a mentor is found. The honoring of the relationship by both the mentor and mentee may, and frequently does, lead to the relationship's expanding as new questions arise. Ultimately the lifelong learning journey of the mentee will lead to new issues for which different mentors will be needed. To the Greek saying "When the student is ready, the teacher will appear," I would now like to add some words of my own: "When the student is ready, the teacher will disappear." All successful mentoring relationships depend on their ending on the same note as they began. The great mentors I have known always seem to know instinctively when the learning they have offered is accomplished and the mentee is ready to move on.

Great mentors prepare the way for the ending of the relationship in the same way that great chess masters are always looking at least three to four moves ahead. For the mentee this process is opaque, and should be, if the ongoing learning process is not to be interrupted before its proper conclusion. Sometimes the ending of the mentor/mentee relationship is tempestuous. Such a risk is inherent in the ending of any relationship deep enough for real learning and partnering to occur. Great mentors may even decide that for the particular mentee, a tempest is the only way for the mentee's spirit to free itself from the relationship so it can move on. No matter how the relationship ends (a bear hug and a wave is certainly better than tears and threats), the mentor and mentee must always be ready to acknowledge, from the relationship's beginning, that the relationship is temporary.

Acknowledging the transitory nature of the relationship at the outset gives the greatest promise for its successful conclusion. For the mentee, awareness that he or she will need many mentors during various stages of his or her journey is a critical part of the relationship. For the mentor, an awareness of the bittersweet role played by an authentic teacher is crucial to the objectivity necessary for the mentee to obtain all the wisdom the mentor can offer. The mentor who can offer all of him or herself to the unique learning process that has led the mentee to choose him or her as mentor, while knowing that eventually the mentee must move on, is the true mentor. Like a parent, the mentor is an intercessor, providing questions and wisdom for life's journey. But mentors are uniquely the persons to whom we grant authority to ask us certain questions that we do not want to answer. Each party must enter the relationship with complete trust, with faith in the possibility of a successful outcome, but without any certainty thereof; and with the profound humility of the novice seeking wisdom and the even profounder humility of the sage who knows how truly little he or she knows.

When I work with families, there are two questions to which I seek answers from each family member at the beginning of our journey together. What are you passionate about, and who is your mentor?

The first question is designed to discover the unique journey to which each individual family member is called. The second question is designed to learn how each family member is pursuing his or her calling, since I am certain that no one can successfully pursue his or her journey of lifelong learning without the mentor needed for each stage of the journey. King Phillip of Macedonia understood this fact when he called on Aristotle to mentor his own son, Alexander. Phillip knew that he had taught Alexander all he could as his father. For the young man to move to the next stage of his journey, he needed a mentor. Little did Phillip know that the mentor he was choosing, Aristotle, would turn the boy not only into a king but into the Emperor of the World, Alexander the Great.

Mentoring is a calling. When seeking mentors, look for one who is called to such a role and who is further called to the unique questions presented by that stage of your life. Be wary of people who suggest they know much. Be attracted to people who, as your intuition will inform you, know much though they profess to know little.

In Closing

To my mentors—

Personally I cannot live without mentors. Beginning with my aunt at age six and the many who have followed, I thank each of them from the depth of my heart. Each of you has made an indelible difference in my self-awareness and thus in my personal journey of happiness. To each, Namaste.

To my readers—

It is my hope that each of you will find, through the courage each of you exhibits, the following in a mentoring relationship:

- the happiness of living on the enlightened plane that a mentorship relationship represents; and
- The way to greater self-awareness and the freedom it brings, as each of you journeys in pursuit of your individual happiness.

Chapter Notes

1. Homer, *The Odyssey,* translated by Robert Fagles (New York: Viking, 1996).

2. Aristotle, *Nicomachean Ethics,* translated by J. A. K. Thomson, revised by Hugh Tredennick (London: Penguin Books, 1953).

3. Paramhansa Yogananda, *The Autobiography of a Yogi* (Los Angeles: Self-Realization Fellowship, 1998).

4. Dante Alighieri, *The Divine Comedy,* translated by Dorothy Sayers (London: Penguin Books, 1949).

5. Shunryu Suzuki, *Zen Mind, Beginner's Mind* (New York: Weatherhill Inc., 2000).

Chapter Eighteen

The Role of Elders

S OME YEARS AGO when I was developing the ideas for this book I tried to establish rules that would parallel the ones that guide the three branches of most democratic governments: legislative, executive, and judicial.

I found it easy to imagine how a family using the idea of all of its adult members serving as a family assembly could develop a legislative branch. I imagined that this branch would have the following responsibilities:

1) Develop the rules for the family's governance and at annual family meetings debate these rules to ensure excellent governance.

2) Vote on the formation of, and candidates for, the family's executive branch, and for the establishment of such other committees and their memberships as would be necessary to achieve the family assembly's goals.

3) Debate and develop the family's mission statement and discuss such changes to it as would ensure that the family's values and goals were clearly defined and were being practiced by all the family's internal and external advisers.

4) Annually review the action of all its representatives to ensure their excellence.

The second branch of family governance, the executive, was also relatively easy to envision. I imagined that in this branch, normally called the family council, representatives of the family as selected by the family assembly would have the following responsibilities:

1) Execute the decisions made by the family assembly in the year following the actions of the family assembly.

2) Select and supervise outside advisers as needed to implement family assembly decisions.

3) Make proposals to the family assembly for such new policies, procedures, and actions as it believed necessary to meet challenges to the family and to its governance system.

4) Be responsible for the nomination of new family council members and for new members of other family committees.

5) Assist with the preparation of the agendas for annual family meetings and for such other meetings of the family or its committees as should be required.

6) Coordinate the preparation of annual family balance sheets, family income statements, and the underlying annual reviews of every family member necessary to compile the information for these family assessment reports.

7) In the event the family assembly adopts a policy of peer reviews, the family council would arrange for such periodic reviews.

8) If the family assembly determines that a family bank or an investor allocation program should be developed for the family, the family executive would arrange for the establishment and operation of these programs.[1]

When I moved to the establishment of a judicial branch, however, I ran into a roadblock. I could not intuit what kind of body I could introduce into a family governance system that could take on the following roles:

1) Effectively deal with internal family disputes.

2) Enforce its judgments on such disputes.

3) Render the advisory opinions to the family needed to ensure that the family's legislative and executive bodies were reflecting the family's values and goals in the process of governance.

4) Tell the family's stories.

The answer lay right under my nose; I simply hadn't looked carefully enough at how my own family works. In our family governance system, we have a family assembly consisting of my parents, my siblings and their spouses and significant others, and the eleven grandchildren and their spouses. We meet annually as an assembly to do the work of the legislative branch. During the year, between meetings, we have a family council acting as the executive branch, which administers the family foundation, a family limited partnership, and whatever other work the assembly assigns to it. On those infrequent occasions (and we as a family are working very hard to keep them infrequent) when a dispute arises among family members, these matters naturally flow up for decision to my parents, and to such other members of the sibling generation as my parents choose to invite to participate with them in resolving the matter. This informal system has served us well during the transition in leadership from my parents' generation to mine and has provided us with a judicial branch of family governance, although at first we didn't recognize it as such.

We have now formally acknowledged that we have a judicial branch, and we call it the council of elders. In addition to dispute resolution, we use the judicial branch of family governance to deepen our sense of our family's differentness, its uniqueness. We ask the elders to remind us at our family meetings of our core values as they pass down to us from prior family generations and through their telling of the family's stories. We ask them to remind us of the seventh-generation wisdom of the Iroquois that "It should be our hope that the care and thoughtfulness we bring to our decision making today will be remembered and honored by our descendants seven generations from today." We ask them to remind us that we are a long-term enterprise endeavoring to preserve our family differentness and thus to "hasten slowly." We have also asked the elders to provide us their wisdom in developing a mission statement for our family's charitable foundation and other business activities. Finally, as we evolve our system of representative family governance, we ask the council of elders to remind us when we don't follow our own rules properly and to assist us, using our core values, in creating new procedures to meet new situations. In each of these roles, the council of elders is performing the role of the judicial branch in family governance.

From the point of view of cultural anthropology, families, as they extend into the third, fourth, fifth, and later generations, become clans and eventually tribes. These family tribes then recreate, as if new, the same basic governance structures that anthropologists have observed are common to all tribes as far back into prehistory as we can infer. In this process, families recognize that as their numbers grow by birth and by marriage, they have a need for greater structure to successfully manage the family's business, whether it lies in the human, intellectual, financial, or social-capital dimensions of the family's activities.

Tribal governance generally consists of elements analogous to the three branches that we have already discussed: an assembly, normally consisting of the adult members of the tribe; an executive or family council, embodied in the chiefs and the medicine men and women; and the council of elders, frequently embodied in the oldest female and sometimes male members of the tribe. Anthropologists often refer to these elder females as "crones."[2] It is not surprising that this role of resolving disputes and holding the tribe to the rules of its governance that have arisen out of its history has so often fallen to the eldest women in the tribe. These women are normally the longest-lived members of the tribe and therefore have the greatest experience of the tribe's history and process of governance. C. G. Jung taught that women, as they age and pass through their change of life, often move from a period of life focused on relationship into a period of power and leadership within society, a process Jung describes as women seeking to integrate their female principle of anima with the male principle of animus.[3] In this light, much of what our society defines as new feminism is not new but is rather the rebirth of the fundamental female role in tribal society—the role of the crone in its governance.

Thinking deeply about the development of a judicial branch can answer two questions posed by many families as they evolve their systems of family governance.

1) As younger-generation family members move toward leadership positions in the family, what should be the current active generation's role in family governance as it becomes the new senior generation?

2) Senior generations should ask, what role can I have in family governance that keeps me active and participating in a way that is appropriate to my seniority but does not cripple the growth and leadership of my children?

These two questions and the answers to them are critical to whether or not a family will make the decisions and take the actions necessary to implement a system of family governance. In my early work with families, I couldn't understand why the family would meet, have excellent discussions, make decisions—and then nothing would happen; the process would never take off. After asking more and more searching questions of these families, I discovered that the above two questions were present in the minds of the two generations called to form the system of family governance. However, the questions were thought too risky to the family dynamic to be voiced. In the parent generation, the parents often feared that if they gave up part of their prior monopoly on family decision making to the family assembly, they would gradually be pushed aside and lose their place and influence. In the children's generation, there was a fear that they would take responsibility as requested by their parents, and then at the first opportunity to actually exercise this authority, their parents would pull the proverbial rug out from under them by vetoing their decisions. When you have both parties to any joint decision making process entering that process with fear about its outcome, rather than positive commitment to its outcome, it is highly unlikely the process will work. In my opinion, for the successful evolution of a judicial branch of family governance, both generations of a family must enter the process of joint decision making with positive enthusiasm. For positive enthusiasm to exist, answers to these two questions and to the fears that underlie them must be found.

I believe the answers lie in defining a role for the parent generation that is appropriate and natural and that reflects the traditional roles of elders that tribal organizations have evolved for their successful governance. If the parent generation feels that it can relinquish day-to-day decision making while retaining a role in the family's longest-term decisions, where its wisdom and knowledge of family tribal history will have their greatest impact, successful generational transitions in family governance can and do occur. The families I work with are proof positive of this, as is my own. The spiritual evolution of the family and the settlement of internal family disputes are two critical areas of family governance where elders can be of immense help. These are roles that the parent generation will immediately see as appropriate to its stage of life and that will usefully employ its wisdom and experience. Appealing to the higher instincts of human beings will always bring out the best in each of us. In this area of family governance, that proposition will work to a family's benefit when it assists the parent generation in using what it considers best about itself as a gift to the future generations of its family.

A family evolving toward joint decision making over a long period of time can help this process significantly if it finds a way—as each generation moves from third to second to first—to capture the wisdom and experience of its forebears. A council of elders, in which to repose the family wisdom and history and from which the resolution of family disputes can flow, offers a place and role in family governance to which all family members can aspire. It offers a recognition to the elders in our family tribes of their usefulness and their critical importance to our families' successful journeys to excellent family governance and to the retarding of the dismal prognosis of the shirtsleeves proverb.

In conclusion, I realize that readers who consider themselves the first or second generation of a family, or who have no earlier living generations, may be wondering, if an inter-generational dispute occurs, how will it serve family governance and the family's joint decision making process if only one generation decides the dispute? Clearly this doesn't seem fair. In general, my remarks assume that a family has enough members of the elder generation to provide objective individuals who are perceived to be able to resolve each dispute. In the event that a particular dispute leaves no elder family member in such an objective position, I recommend that the parties then choose an elder from within the learned professions or from another family to whom they are closely related or aligned to act in this capacity. The settling of such a dispute should be viewed by the family as exceptional and in no way limiting to the future role of the family's council of elders in all of its other important functions, including the settling of other disputes.

My wish and hope are that your family will use all of its human and intellectual assets to their greatest potential. In this process, it is my hope that you will especially honor the gifts of wisdom and knowledge of tribal history that flow from your elders, and that you will find a proper place within the judicial branch of your system of family governance to repose these invaluable treasures.

Chapter Notes

1. Investor allocation and the family bank are discussed in detail in Chapters 5 and 7.

2. One of the best books on this role is *The Crone: Women of Age, Wisdom and Power,* by Barbara Walker (Harper, 1998).

3. For readers interested in these phenomena, Gail Sheehy's two books on male and female developmental changes, *New Passages: Mapping Your Life Across Time* (Ballantine Books, 1996) and *Passages: Predictable Crises of Adult Life* (Bantam, 1977), are insightful.

Chapter Nineteen

The Trustee as Mentor

E VERY DAY, SOMEWHERE in the world a human being who is cast in the role of beneficiary of a trust accuses her or his trustee of being unresponsive to her or his request to be heard and to be represented. From this accusation (all too often true!) flow at least distress and disappointment and at worst litigation. How can a trust set up by one human being to benefit another come to such a tragic place? Easily, when we understand that the relationship between the trustee and the beneficiary is an arranged marriage.[1]

Since the beginning of the use of trusts in the Middle Ages, very few, if any, beneficiaries have chosen their trustees. Founders, grantors, settlors, whatever term we use (hereinafter I will use grantor), select the trustees of the trusts they create. Grantors of inter vivos revocable trusts (who are also the beneficiaries of such trusts) select the trustees for the new trusts that often grow out of their original trusts at their deaths. Grantors of all irrevocable trusts select the trustees of the trusts they create. Whether a trust becomes irrevocable by inter vivos deed or by death, it is the grantor who seeks, interviews, and selects the trustee. The beneficiary and the trustee, from the date of the trust's irrevocability forward, "for richer or for poorer, until death [or divorce, i.e. litigation] do them part," are irrevocably related.

Unfortunately for this relationship, arranged marriages have not been in vogue for some time. Even in the East they are beginning to be seen as an antique idea. Why? Because human beings believe that if they are going to give up any part of their freedom of action, it must be because the reward of doing so is perceived as being of greater value than the loss of freedom it requires. It is in the choosing that this balancing of risk and reward is carried out. It is the right to choose the party to the new relationship that makes the giving up of freedom possible. To be sure, the choice may be a poor one and the relationship may fail, but the responsibility for the outcome is accepted by the chooser. With choice comes responsibility for the relationship and for participating in it. In the beneficiary/trustee relationship, no reciprocal choice by the beneficiary takes place. The beneficiary is not invested with responsibility for the relationship or participation in it. The trustee does have some investment in the relationship, since the person named as trustee, whether individual or corporate, agreed to accept the role of trustee and the legal responsibilities associated with it.

Many trustees are not introduced to their new partner, the beneficiary, until the "wedding night" (following the signing of the trust agreement by the trust's grantor or on the grantor's death), and at this point a new relationship has to be formed. Unfortunately for most of these new beneficiary/trustee relationships, rarely do the parties understand that the human relationship they are entering will be far more important to the trust's success than the proper maintenance of their legal relationship. How quickly the trustee and beneficiary come to grips with this truth and begin to manage this human relationship will have a profound impact on how beneficial the trust will prove to be for both parties.

How can the beneficiary and trustee begin this relationship with the greatest possibility of success? Shortly, I will discuss some principles that excellent beneficiaries and excellent trustees must accept and fulfill for a successful relationship. For now, let me simply say that every individual or corporation considering accepting the role of trustee must comprehend and be willing to do three things:

1) understand that in agreeing to become a trustee, he or she is entering into a human relationship with the beneficiary, not just a legal one;

2) do everything in his or her power to get to know the potential beneficiary of the trust before the implementation of the trust; and

3) appreciate from the first meeting with the beneficiary that this relationship is an arranged marriage.

There is a second significant roadblock to a successful relationship between the trustee and the beneficiary. It is the failure of the grantor of the trust to perceive that in order for the recipient to have her or his life enhanced rather than depreciated by a gift, the recipient—the beneficiary of the trust—must believe that she or he is worthy of such a gift. We all know how disempowering gifts, or handouts, from the government have proven to be for the least privileged in our society. Why should we believe that the beneficiary of a trust is any different? In psychology, a new disease has been defined. It is called "remittance addiction." Every trust officer and every individual trustee lives with the knowledge that a poorly administered trust will result in this syndrome. What can be more disempowering to a human being than becoming dependent on, and waiting anxiously for, the check on the first of the month? Obviously, I am not speaking of people with physical or mental disabilities. I am speaking of trust beneficiaries who are perfectly able, physically and mentally, but who are as dependent on trust remittances as others are on drugs or alcohol.

Dependence creates all kinds of behavior; none are behavior choices free people make. Why do trusts carry this risk? First, many privileged families have been given no early warning messages by their trusted advisers that this problem exists. This is especially true in the families of first-generation entrepreneurs where there has been no historic experience with significant wealth or with trusts. Second, the largest number of trusts created each year are created for tax purposes. In my experience, most of these trusts are created without any careful thought being given to the beneficiary/trustee relationship and particularly to the issue of whether the beneficiary will consider herself or himself worthy of the gift. Tax planning is a necessity for families with wealth and must be carried out with excellence. However, over the time periods of one hundred years or more that are considered in this book, the tax planning of today will turn out to be barely relevant. A family's successful wealth preservation is in jeopardy if the family beneficiaries, the family's critical wealth, and its human capital are "remittance addicted" and are quickly taking the family out of business. A gift made principally for tax purposes has no life in it for the human beings who are supposed to be benefited. They will properly ask the trustee, "Why was I given this gift? Why am I worthy of it?" Only trouble will follow for a trustee who says "Because Grandpa loved you" when the trustee knows that Grandpa was actually more anxious to take something away from the tax collector than to give something to the beneficiary. The trustee's answer must be the truth, or the beneficiary will find the truth on his or her own and will never trust the trustee again. All too often the truth is that Grandpa wanted to take it with him, but since he could not and since the tax man was there, Grandpa decided to set up a monument to himself that would remind later generations of his family of his success as a wealth creator. In many instances, Grandpa really did not care about the impact of the gift on the beneficiary.

So here we have the trustee and the beneficiary in an arranged marriage where the beneficiary often will discover that the question of his or her personal worthiness to be in this relationship was never considered. Necessarily, this fact leaves the beneficiary in a quandary as to how to view the trust and his or her role in it. There are frequently many other unresolved issues of worthiness between the grantor and the beneficiary, too specific to each family fact pattern for me to discuss here. I will, however, quote my father, who taught me at the beginning of my legal career that "If at a grantor's death he or she has left unresolved issues in a relationship with the beneficiary of a trust, death in no way will resolve these issues but rather will leave the beneficiary behind to try to answer unanswerable questions." These questions will surface between the beneficiary and the trustee. How the trustee reacts to them will have a great deal to do with the success of the beneficiary/trustee relationship and whether the beneficiary feels worthy of the gift of the trust or falls into "remittance addiction."

I imagine many of you by now are disagreeing with me. You may be saying, "I know many grantors whose trusts were created as gifts of pure love and who had every intention that the beneficiary's life be improved and empowered by the gift." Happily, I too represent many such grantors. My larger experience, however, has taught me that they are not the grantors whose gifts lead to the need for this chapter. To the contrary, they and their families are the models who have taught me the lessons I am sharing with you about how to become an excellent beneficiary or an excellent trustee and how to forge an excellent beneficiary/trustee relationship.

I propose that the solution to a successful beneficiary/trustee relationship lies in the trustee's offering and the beneficiary's accepting the proposition that at the inception of the trust, the trustee's role is to be the beneficiary's mentor, and the trustee will remain in that role until the beneficiary is fully participating in the beneficiary/trustee relationship, at which time the trustee's role will evolve into that of the beneficiary's representative. In all relationships that are successful learning experiences for both participants, the party with more knowledge at the beginning must offer that knowledge in such a way that the party with less knowledge willingly assumes the role of pupil. Then, as we saw in Chapter 17, when the student is ready, the teacher will know when to disappear.

In a beneficiary/trustee relationship, normally the trustee has the knowledge, both human and legal, of how the relationship is meant to work. The beneficiary normally does not. If the trustee at the outset of this relationship offers to mentor the beneficiary until he or she can achieve excellence, as discussed below, and if the beneficiary experiences the trustee's offer as true and as a gift, their relationship has an excellent chance of being successful.

Unfortunately, all too often, the trustee sees excellence as limited to investment and administrative success. The trustee fails to perceive that what he or she knows about the human and legal nature of the beneficiary/trustee relationship must be communicated to and learned and assimilated by the beneficiary if their relationship is to be a success. Even more unfortunate for a successful beneficiary/trustee relationship is the situation where the trustee wonders why this beneficiary who seems so intelligent in many areas of life seems so dense about a subject the trustee considers to be so simple. Why should this question even arise in a trustee's mind? All too often, in my experience, the trustee is a person or institution with excellent quantitative skills but little or no experience or training in qualitative issues. Meanwhile, the beneficiary is often a person with excellent qualitative skills who lacks experience in quantitative issues. Like the failures in communication between science and the humanities, it is not surprising that beneficiaries and trustees making fundamentally different journeys in life find it hard to understand one another.[2] If a trustee can recognize this mismatch and transcend it by offering to mentor the beneficiary so that she or he can learn and then exercise her or his role in the trust, their relationship stands a chance of harmony. Trustees who fail to learn at the outset of the trust what the beneficiaries do and don't understand about their relationship, or worse, assume the beneficiaries know all that's necessary "since, after all, this stuff is so simple anyone should understand it," do so at their peril.

To be asked to be a mentor is the highest honor that can be bestowed by one human on another. When selecting a trustee, the grantor of a trust is well advised to consider the potential trustee's ability to mentor the beneficiaries he or she loves as the highest qualification among all of the many things a trustee must do. If a trustee is an excellent administrator, a superb and prudent investor, and a Solomonic and humane distributor but is perceived by the beneficiary to be distant, aloof, and unable to communicate in a way the beneficiary can understand, their relationship will be unsuccessful. It is in the role of mentor that a trustee's real worth to the beneficiary, and thus to the grantor's desire to make a gift that is empowering to the beneficiary, can be found.

In my original proposition, I suggest that the trustee's relationship with the beneficiary must evolve from mentor to representative. The term representative suggests a form of governance. Trusts contain within their terms systems of governance. After all, whenever two or more persons are in any relationship, they must make joint decisions. Joint decision making means that the parties are in a system of governance. In the beneficiary/trustee system of governance, the trustee is the representative of the beneficiary, because it is to him or her that the trustee is accountable. If the trustee makes unilateral decisions and imposes them on a beneficiary who has no choice but to accept them, in political science terms we have a tyranny. When called to account, tyrants historically have not fared well. If the trustee makes joint decisions but always exercises the deciding vote, the beneficiary will quickly determine that there is no purpose in dealing with the trustee and opt out by silence or anger. If the trustee and the beneficiary make joint decisions, and the beneficiary has been mentored by the trustee and has become an equal party to the representative system of governance, the trustee will almost never have to exercise a deciding vote. The beneficiary will know that even if the trustee makes a decision with which he or she disagrees, the trustee is acting as his or her representative and the decision is likely to be a fair one.

It is my contention that the beneficiary/trustee system of governance works best when the trustee evolves from mentor to representative, and thus the system of governance becomes a republic—the same model I have proposed for governance within families. This system of beneficiary/trustee governance permits each party the greatest freedom, the greatest chance of mutual respect, and ultimately, the greatest trust. It would seem to me that every trustee, knowing that one day accounts must be rendered, will want the beneficiary judging these accounts to receive them in a spirit of mutual respect and trust. The alternative is the antithesis of trust and is symbolic of no "trust" ever having existed.

In Conclusion

I believe that the beneficiary/trustee relationship, if it follows principles of joint learning based on mutual trust and respect, can be an extraordinarily successful one for both parties. It can offer to each a fulfilling role in long-term wealth preservation planning for the beneficiary.

However, unless the trustee accepts a role as the beneficiary's mentor and ultimate representative, the trust may never achieve the success the grantor hoped for when he or she created it as a gift of love and as a gift of hope for the enhancement of the beneficiary's individual pursuit of happiness.

To help grantors and beneficiaries see clearly how to measure an excellent trustee, I close with a picture showing ascending levels of trustee excellence.

The first level represents an excellent quantitative trustee who fulfills all the legal requirements. The second level represents a trustee who in addition to excelling at the first level provides, when requested, the education the beneficiary seeks. The highest level, trustee as mentor, represents a trustee who proactively seeks out the beneficiary to provide both quantitative and qualitative excellence. As I have stated earlier, the title of mentor is the highest honor one human being can bestow on another. For a trustee to be so honored by a beneficiary is to achieve true excellence.

To each beneficiary and to each trustee who sets out on the journey to achieve excellence in this complex relationship, I salute your courage and trust that your journey together will be crowned with success.

Chapter Notes

1. Portions of this chapter were originally published in slightly different form in *The Chase Journal* (Volume II, Issue 2, Spring 1998).

2. For a helpful guide to the different ways we learn, refer to Daniel P. Goleman's book *Emotional Intelligence: Why It Can Matter More Than IQ* (New York: Bantam Books, 1995).

Chapter Twenty

The Trustee as Regent

This chapter was jointly written with Patricia M. Angus, whose help over many years has been invaluable.

THIS REFLECTION EXPLORES how a trust (referred to in the singular, although a family may, and probably will, use more than one trust) fits into the system of family governance. In my experience, although many families have relied upon trusts for the purpose of managing and disposing of their wealth, the most successful ones understand that the term or life span of a trust represents a period of regency within the representative governance system created by the family.

Traditionally, the term regency has been used to describe a period during which a king, or other leader, is unable to rule due to minority, prolonged absence, or a disability, such as mental incompetence. A trust is essentially a period of regency, as it represents a time during which the full ownership of property is suspended. During this interval of suspension of ownership, the trustee takes possession of property from the prior owner and holds the property for the benefit of the beneficiaries, who, at some point or at several points over a period of time as set forth in the trust agreement, will become the next owners of the property.

One need not dig too deeply into the history books to find numerous examples of periods of regency, especially in the history of government. Although the most notable examples are found in the history of monarchies, the experiences are nonetheless relevant to the representative system that I consider the preferable family governance system. Often, a prince has become king before attaining an age at which he is able to exercise his powers, or has been required to be away from the seat of government for prolonged periods, such as during war. The most well-known regencies in Western history are the leadership of England's King John during the imprisonment of Richard the Lion-Hearted, and the stewardship of France by Philippe II, duc d'Orléans, during the minority of Louis XV. In each of these periods, the rightful king was unable to rule; as a result, his closest relatives were selected to perform his duties until the disability ended.

History tells us that the regency of John was a period of chaos in England, leading to the famous story of Robin Hood, while the regency of Philippe II was a period of general success and order in France. In Richard's case, the period ended with the payment of ransom for his return; for Louis XV, his attainment of the age of majority terminated the regency. When Richard died, John assumed the kingship and was such a poor king that he was forced, after losing a war to his barons, to sign the Magna Carta, and thus gave away substantial portions of his power. Louis, on the other hand, with careful guidance by his uncle on how to become a king, ruled through most of the eighteenth century. During this period, France retained its position as a great power in Europe, and Philippe II died peacefully in his bed.

These two historic patterns have much to teach us about the trustee's role as a regent. The creation of a trust by a family member, or members, commences a period of regency in a family governance system. In much the same way as Philippe duc d'Orléans or King John assumed a set of rights, responsibilities, and obligations as regent, so too must the trustee oversee and manage the trust property and nurture a relationship with trust beneficiaries to ensure a successful regency period.

What are some of the things a trustee, in this capacity as regent, can do to help ensure that the period is prosperous for all involved, so that there will be a satisfactory conclusion of the regency when the trust property is turned over to the beneficiaries?

We propose that certain characteristics of successful periods of regency in the governmental context provide a model for the success of a regency in the family governance system. These characteristics are as follows:

- *The trustee must, of course, focus on the education of the beneficiaries to prepare them for the ultimate ownership of the property.* This responsibility always transcends all other duties of a regent, who is primarily responsible for preparing the sovereign for future leadership. This duty, performed excellently by the trustee, assures that the trust will prove to be a contributing asset. It will aid in the preparation of the beneficiaries for the possibility of lives in which they will successfully pursue individual journeys of happiness. While the trust cannot assure the outcome of these journeys, the trustee–regent, acting as mentor, can seek to assure that the beneficiaries will not become "remittance addicted." The mentoring trustee can thus also be a powerful force in working to overcome the psychological issues of dependence that arise from lack of ownership and that frequently have made trusts counterproductive in the lives of their beneficiaries. A trustee who fails to address the education of the beneficiaries as owners fails the highest obligation to the founder of the trust, which is to create educated owners of the trust assets.

- *Trustees must earn their authority, and they cannot take their position of power for granted.* A regent cannot successfully act in the place of the appointed king unless the regent has the respect and loyalty of the king's subjects. Without this, there is a danger of debilitating conflict, despotism, or anarchy. The trustee must understand the issues that "control without ownership" present in the family governance system (see Chapter 9). All too often the trustee assumes that ownership constitutes control. In fact, for a trust to be successfully governed for the benefit of the beneficiaries, it is necessary for the trustee to understand that he or she is no more, and no less, than the representative of the beneficiaries.

- *The regent must be responsible to all beneficiaries, whether current or future, in accordance with the provisions of the trust.* In a monarchy and in family governance, there is a real danger that a regent or trustee can abuse his or her power by favoring certain individuals, generations, or groups over others. In government, the regent must be aware of the conflicting needs of all citizens and would favor court insiders over the general public only at great risk to the regency and the state. The trustee must adhere closely to the founder's wishes and must at all times weigh and balance competing interests (often between income beneficiaries and remaindermen) in light of the provisions of the trust. Like the regent, the trustee is accountable to the beneficiaries and will receive praise or blame for the actions taken during the period of suspended ownership when the trusteeship comes to an end. Woe to a trustee who, like King John, must explain to the beneficiary why the affairs of state are in chaos. Praise to the trustee who, like the regent Philippe II duc d'Orléans, turns over the entrusted property to the beneficiary with its affairs in reasonable order.

- *The trustee must always subordinate his or her own interests to those of the beneficiaries.* While it is obvious that a king's uncle, while serving as regent, cannot raid the treasury for his own purposes without risking disaster for himself and the state, it is also important for a trustee to remember that the beneficiaries' interests always supersede his or her own. On the most basic level, trustees cannot under any circumstances use trust property for their own needs or purposes. This does not mean that a trustee cannot receive reasonable compensation for his or her services or reimbursement of expenses. Trustees or regents violate the governance system, however, if they take advantage of their position as legal owner of the property to improve their own position.

- *The trustee must possess the necessary skills and expertise to properly perform the tasks required under the trust.* Obviously, it would be quite dangerous for a regent to assume control of a country without any background or experience in government. Too often, this is forgotten in choosing a trustee. A close, warm relationship with the trust founder cannot be considered a substitute for the expertise required of an excellent trustee. Investment experience, administrative skills, and a sense of diplomacy are just some of the skills that a successful trustee must possess.

- *Trustees must always remember that their ownership of the property is only temporary.* In all periods of regency, there is a moment of transition when the regent, as surrogate leader, must transfer the reins of government to the king or queen, as rightful sovereign. From the beginning, the trustee must always be prepared to cede ownership to the beneficiaries at a moment's notice, should the period of the trust's life come to an end or through an early termination of the trust upon completion of its terms. The trustee must be mindful of the fact that exerting so much power over something that ultimately must be released is a difficult yet empowering position. Each trustee must understand and be ever mindful of the provisional nature of his or her relationship to the trust property. From the beginning, the trustee must be preparing to let go.

• *The trustee must strive to maintain open and honest communication with the beneficiaries.* A regent must obtain information on the needs and circumstances of all citizens to understand fully the government's obligations to ensure the welfare of its subjects. As a representative of the beneficiaries, the trustee must make every effort to know the beneficiaries intimately in order to represent them fully. In this relationship, the trustee and the beneficiaries will mutually form the policies that will best carry out the trust's mission and prepare the beneficiaries for ownership.

• *The regent must know when to relinquish power and how to effectively transfer it to the rightful beneficiaries.* A regent should not, indeed cannot, overstay his or her welcome as the surrogate leader. Even if the trust provisions do not provide a single moment at which full ownership and control of the property is to be transferred to the beneficiaries, the trustee must be willing to admit when it is time to hand over power. The transfer is usually to the beneficiaries but sometimes to a successor trustee who is more suited to the task. Once decided, the trustee must discuss carefully with the beneficiaries the logistics of transferring the property and in what form they wish to receive it.

Comprehending the trustee's role as mentor and the trust's characteristic as a period of regency brings the reality of this complex legal arrangement into clearer focus for trustee and beneficiary alike. Too often, the trustee is seen only as a prudent investor, competent administrator, and humane distributor. There is no doubt that these trustee functions are important, and if not performed excellently will lead to negative consequences for the trust and its beneficiaries. However, even if these functions are performed brilliantly, a trustee's failure to understand his or her most important role—that of mentor—and the trust's most important characteristic—that of a period of regency in the family governance system—will lead to a failure to realize the ultimate goal: development of the beneficiaries as the eventual owners of the trust assets.

The trustee's full participation in the family governance system assures the suspended owners of the trust property the representation in that governance system that they deserve while they are waiting to assume actual ownership. When trustees fail to understand their role as regent and their responsibility to develop excellent beneficiaries as owners, they do not meet their duty toward the founder's gift of love in creating the trust—a gift given to enhance the capacity of each beneficiary to pursue individual happiness and to achieve a useful and fulfilled life.

Chapter Twenty-One

Unexpected Consequences of a Perpetual Trust

D URING THE LAST dozen years, many attorneys and financial planners in the United States have recommended that
their clients create perpetual trusts. These vehicles are frequently
referred to as dynasty trusts. While there are a number of individual
and family reasons that might impel an individual to create such a
trust, in large measure the motivating factor has been to avoid the
federal generation-skipping tax on the assets of trusts for later family generations.[1]

This method of tax avoidance has created a cottage industry in
perpetual trusts. This industry has now reached sufficient scale that
a number of states interested in competing for this business have
eliminated their rules against perpetuities to permit the creation of
perpetual trusts within their boundaries. (In doing so, they joined
a number of states that had never adopted this rule.) These new
statutes are overturning some three-hundred-plus years of statutes
and common-law precedents in England and America that were
founded on the principle that trusts for individuals, as opposed to
charities, should not be permitted to last indefinitely.

It is my observation that this emphasis on tax saving as the
motive for the creation of perpetual trusts, and the resulting
changes in statutory and precedentual law to meet this motive, have
frequently obscured critical thinking by planners and trust founders

on how the lives of the beneficiaries living within such trusts will be affected and of how society as a whole may view the existence of such trusts. I would like to illuminate these issues here so that planners and founders may consider them in determining how the perpetual trusts they are intending to create will be of the greatest benefit to the individuals for whom the trusts are created.

The trust as we know it evolved in England and on the European continent, particularly in France, out of the Roman idea of "use." This is the legal concept that provides that a person may have the use of a thing for a period of time without also having the underlying ownership of that thing. This idea took root in the English and French common laws as the trust, and by the time of the Crusades it was well established in land titles. At that time the law made no distinction regarding the terms of trusts, thus permitting trusts to last indefinitely or, if you will, perpetually. Rather quickly, the nobility of England and France saw that by placing their lands in perpetual trusts they could, theoretically, perpetuate their class position indefinitely. Therefore, much of England and France's land found its way into perpetual trusts.[2]

Unfortunately for the economics of the countries where this system developed, there were two unintended consequences. First, the land in trust often could not be alienated even if the noble family needed money or in some cases had disappeared. Second, such lands were often poorly administered, because they had no owner who cared about their improvement, since he or she would never own them outright. Many life tenants sought to receive the maximum annual return possible without regard to such a policy's long-term effect on the land's productivity.

The result of these unintended consequences was that a portion of England's and France's wealth was seen by its rising commercial classes to be wasted. Equally, those who had money and entrepreneurial creativity were frustrated that they could not buy and improve this land, thus exacerbating the perceived negative effect of the perpetual trust on the economy. In addition, the suspension of vesting of property as a result of perpetual trusts often led to certain members or even whole generations of noble families becoming trust-funders and falling into the same lassitude or remittance addiction that we often see today in some of the third- and fourth-generation members of the great families of nineteenth-century Industrial America. Often then, as now, this lassitude resulted from the fact that no member of that noble family ever owned or would own the capital locked up in the trust from which he or she received monthly stipends, nor would any family member ever be required to learn to manage these assets. In fact, work in commerce of any kind was seen as beneath the dignity of such personages.

The result of these perpetual trusts in England was that, by the end of the seventeenth century, the perpetual trust came to be seen by lawyers, merchants, and economists as a substantial drag on commerce (since so much land could not be purchased or sold) and as an abuse of the original idea of trust: that a period of suspension of ownership while another used something could be beneficial to commerce. The result of these concerns was the adoption in England, in the late 1600s, of the Rule Against Perpetuities. At the time this rule was adopted, first by case law and then by statute, lawyers, judges, economists, and parliamentarians saw it as a great reform.[3]

The history of the perpetual trust in France is also instructive. Historically, France had a well-understood perpetual trust provision. Until its revolution in 1789, France made no such reform as the English made with their Rule Against Perpetuities. In France the absence of such a reform and the resulting restriction on the growth of France's economy, caused by the inability to purchase and sell land, slowed France's development. The perceived abuse of the economy, through the use of the perpetual trust by the nobility, was seen by Napoleon and the jurists who advised him to be so serious that in 1805, in the Code Napoléon, he eliminated the trust altogether in France. Today a number of French lawyers are attempting to reintroduce the trust through a legal entity called the *fiducie*, because they feel the lack of this vehicle has held back their clients' ability to properly plan their estates. None of the advocates of the *fiducie*, interestingly, are suggesting such an entity be perpetual.

So what can we learn from the history of the perpetual trusts? We can say that at least at one time in the evolution of the law of trusts, such trusts were perceived by society to have had a significant negative impact on the marketplace and to have perpetuated a non-productive class of people. As to the first of society's objections to the perpetual trust, there is no doubt about such trusts' historically negative impact on land sales and acquisitions. As to the second, the histories of France and Russia have not been kind to a class of people whom society perceives as never needing to earn their own living, and particularly unkind to those who enjoy such a status just because an ancestor, whom they often never even knew, created a perpetual trust for his or her descendants.

There is a third drawback to the perpetual character of dynasty trusts, a disadvantage less widely perceived in the society at large but pertinent to our modern economic environment, where wealth is represented far more in movable assets than in immovable property. The trustees of nearly every trust are constrained by the state laws that govern trusts to make no investment that is not prudent. In the commercial arena, however, creativity is defined as entrepreneur-ship and is all about taking risks. Creativity and the risks it entails are not included within these state-law definitions of prudence, and rightly so, since it is someone else's assets that the trustee is adminis-tering. This reality proves unfortunate over time for trust beneficia-ries. Why? Because over time, the prudent trustee cannot take the risks that an entrepreneur using his or her own resources can take, and so, over time, the return achieved by the trustee in competition with all other investors will be less. This logic, carried out over the multiple generations assumed by a perpetual trust, suggests strongly that, assuming the market is neutral, a trust's assets will fail to grow at the same rate as the market as a whole, and suggests that such trusts will eventually find themselves in the same negative position commercially as those that owned but could not trade in land.

When I address the supposedly new idea of a perpetual trust, I am reminded of the admonition by George Santayana that "those who cannot remember the past are condemned to repeat it." I won-der how many of the multitude of financial planners who promote dynasty trusts as a product and rush them off the shelf to solve a tax problem have studied the history of the first chapters in the life of the perpetual trust. I wonder how many of them understand that many previous societies have found the creation of a perpetual leisure class unacceptable, and that the longer assets remain prudently invested within a trust, the greater the likelihood that those assets will underperform the market as a whole. It is my purpose in this chapter to raise these questions so that we as planners can meet the wise man's admonition about remembering the past and form a thoughtful view about perpetual trusts. By doing so we can best advise our clients on the possible outcomes of the plans they are creating. I also feel obliged to observe that the United States Congress in 2001 passed the Economic Growth and Tax Relief Reconciliation, which will eliminate the federal generation-skipping tax. I wonder whether greater familiarity with the history of the perpetual trust, and with the issues I am about to discuss of beneficiaries' lives within such trusts, might have caused many founders to pause and think before creating a perpetual legal vehicle, especially had they not been driven to solve a tax problem that may very well not exist for the trust's lifetime.

Let us look, then, at three issues that would not normally be first thoughts in the minds of tax planners but are often the first thoughts of caring professionals concerned about the long-term effects of their actions on the lives of their clients, on the families of which they are a part, and on the systems within which they live and operate. Let us consider the law of unintended or unexpected consequences; the interest of society in the outcomes of the individual decisions of its members, and society's ability to influence these decisions; and the second law of thermodynamics, the law of entropy.

The Law of Unexpected Consequences

Modern physics informs us that there are often unintended or unexpected consequences of acts the universe performs. Increasingly, modern economists, social scientists, and psychologists are seeing this same reality and applying these principles in their fields. The ancient Greeks understood this idea long before its modern disciples and expressed it when they were preparing young men and women to enter the service professions, by admonishing them to do no harm. The ancient Greeks recognized that rushing to do good before understanding the whole system and all the issues relating to the problem to be solved often led to doing more harm than good.

I would synthesize modern thinkers and the Greeks by suggesting that because there are often unintended or unexpected consequences of what we do, and because some of what we do may do harm, we should start any planning project with the rule "First, be sure to do no harm." This rule is particularly applicable to the creation of a perpetual trust. Why? Because the planner is mortal, and the trust he or she is creating is theoretically immortal. In such a case, many questions regarding the natures and experiences of the descendants of the trust's founder, and the environment in which they and the trust will exist, will not only not be known or discernable by the founder, they will also not be known or discernable by the planner. The planner, in assisting the founder in creating such a trust, must recognize that he or she will be significantly affecting the lives of each of the trustee's beneficiaries, as each beneficiary in turn integrates the trust's existence into his or her own. It can be a humbling experience for trust planners and trust founders to imagine what life might be like for these beneficiaries even just two or three generations removed from those alive today, much less the seventh, eighth, and ninth, generations thereafter. Perhaps the admonition of the Iroquois elders to one another as they began important tribal work—"It should be our hope that the care and thoughtfulness we bring to our decision making today will be remembered and honored by our descendants seven generations from today"—would be helpful to planners and founders of perpetual trusts as they begin their work. Rightly, the creation of a perpetual trust, affecting so many generations of a family, ought to be done and entered into with great humility and plenty of patience. The thought "hasten slowly" comes again to mind.

I strongly suggest that every planner carefully consider all the possible impacts the trust may have on the lives of its beneficiaries, particularly its unintended consequences, and bring those thoughts to the attention of the trust's potential founder. By so alerting the trust's founder, the planner will be trying to eliminate to the greatest extent possible the negative impact the trust might have on these beneficiaries, and to meet an adviser's highest responsibility to the founder and the beneficiaries to do no harm. Strangely, I often observe that in the rush to get the tax work done and the papers out, the trust's impact on the lives of its beneficiaries is never discussed. This failure to take the time to consider these issues may be, from the founder's standpoint, given his or her intention to benefit the beneficiaries by enhancing their lives, the greatest unintended mistake. Why? Because it may lead to the creation of a trust that diminishes the lives of its beneficiaries. Should such a result occur, the founder would have been deprived by the trust's planner of the advice he or she most needed in attempting to accomplish his or her enhancement goals.

We as planners owe a duty to our clients to bring to them all the issues that may impact their decisions so that they may make the most informed decisions. It is my hope that when one of our clients is thinking of creating a perpetual trust, such issues as its possible negative impact on its beneficiaries by (1) causing them to become remittance addicted, or worse, victims of the state of mind we know as entitlement, and (2) depriving them of a chance to dream and the freedom to bring their dreams to life will be the issues we choose to discuss most deeply with the founder. Why? Because in these issues lies the greatest risk of unintended negative consequences to the lives of the beneficiaries and to the enhancement goals of the trust's founder.

Society and the Perpetual Trust

Turning to the second of my questions, society's interest in the decisions its individual members make: as I explained previously, English, French, and Russian societies at earlier periods of history found the perpetual trust and the perpetual-leisure or nonworking class it created unacceptable. In America, anxiety about the existence of such a class led to the adoption, first by inheritance of the English common law and later by individual state statutes, of rules against perpetuities. These statutes expressed society's view that the perpetual suspension of the ownership of property was an unacceptable hindrance to the economy and to the movement of wealth within society as a whole. These rules may also express a concern about a perpetually landed class that did not need to work.

My aim here is simply to point out to planners that in France and arguably Russia, enmity toward a landed class helped lead to revolution. I believe it is our duty as planners to advise our clients of these histories so that they may consider all points of view before acting to create an entity that certain societies have seen as unacceptable. I believe it is also important to consider that no society known to history has ever accepted within its midst a perpetually leisured or nonworking class.

As a historian and amateur sociologist, I cringe when I see masterful statistical analyses created by trust planners projecting the enormous buildups of wealth within these perpetual trust entities, all designed to encourage potential trust founders to get on with buying such a product from the planner. I wonder whether the planner is appealing to the founder's ego by suggesting the creation of such a monument to the founder, all the while disguising this fact by suggesting how happy the beneficiaries will be.[4] History shows that society has never permitted such monuments to last very long. Remember Ozymandias? I suggest that society, like biology, seeks creation and change in order to meet new circumstances and to allow new forms of community to arise. As Heraclitus said, everything is in flux. I suggest that society dislikes the profound order found in monuments. Given this history, I suggest that society's concerns have to be taken into account in characterizing to founders the long-term likelihood that their planners' projections of monumental financial results will turn out to be true. I also caution readers who are now just beginning to imagine life without federal estate taxation and federal generation-skipping taxation to consider how likely it is that American society will bring both of these taxes back if it perceives that they are needed as a way to avoid a perpetual-leisure or nonworking class. Coming again to the law of unintended consequences, are we, as planners, recreating the environment within American society for the re-enactment of the federal estate tax and generation-skipping tax sometime in the future by promulgating perpetual trusts?

The Law of Entropy

Finally, we have the third issue: the second law of thermodynamics, or the law of entropy. This law of physics reminds us that everything that is material will over time be frictioned away by entropy. While it may be heartening to trust founders to think they are perpetually endowing the enhancement of the lives of their descendants, I strongly suggest that they be disabused of such an idea. Planners who play to the hubris of their clients by suggesting that a perpetual trust is a monument that will endure forever are pandering to their clients' worst instincts. Bringing the law of entropy into the conversation brings both planner and founder back to humility and to the awareness that in their work together on a legal entity that will impact others lives—and particularly a perpetual trust, with its intended extended period of life—they must be sure *they will do no harm before they try to do good.*

Summing up this section, I cannot urge too strongly that planners discuss with potential founders of perpetual trusts the following three important realities:

1) There will be unintended consequences of this perpetual trust. Have we considered as many possible outcomes of the creation of this trust as we can imagine, with our greatest focus being on those that may decrease, rather than increase, the pursuits of individual happiness of the beneficiaries of the trust? Have we used the seventh-generation wisdom of the Iroquois? Have we hastened slowly? Have we asked what harm will we do before we try to do good?

2) Society will have a view about (and an impact on) this perpetual trust. Have we considered what society's view and impact might be? Have we considered not only that society is averse to what we may first perceive as our goal of having a trust last perpetually but also that society may have a valid point of view that might cause us to modify our plan? Have we at least considered the idea that society as a system will in some way constrain our goals of having a trust last perpetually?

3) *The law of entropy is alive and well and informs us that nothing material lasts forever.* Have we brought this law of physics into our consciousness as we plan, and have we imagined how it will impact the life and operation of the perpetual trust?

The emphasis of the three areas set out above appears to be on external forces that will affect a perpetual trust. I argue, however, that the most significant risk to the success of a perpetual trust is internal. It is the risk that because of a lack of internal governance of the relationship between the beneficiaries and the trustees, the trust will not enhance the lives of its beneficiaries but rather will diminish them. One is reminded of Walt Kelly's comic character Pogo, who went searching for the enemy and found it was us. In other words, a trust's planners, founders, and beneficiaries are the most likely cause of the trust's failure to prove enhancing to its beneficiaries. In my practice, it is common to meet beneficiaries who tell me that a trust has been a net negative in their lives.

Planners who are seeking genuinely to guide their clients will always offer them an enlightened and educated view of the possible outcome of trusts. The sharing of such views is particularly important in the case of perpetual trusts. Why? Because the laws of demographic probability imply a geometric increase in the possible beneficiaries of such trusts in each later family generation. Thus, through the normal birth rates expected within families, such trusts are more likely to spawn unproductive or remittance-addicted persons than are fixed-term trusts. The potential founders of perpetual trusts are entitled to be made aware of this potential.

Another reality of trusts of all kinds is that many beneficiaries do not feel worthy of such a gift and find the trust a hindrance to their development, to their sense of freedom to make their own life choices, and to their sense of self-worth. While to the average person without a trust these may seem like strange thoughts, they are in fact one of the realities of trust life. Many beneficiaries feel that the trust saps them of creativity and the excitement of making something of their own. They sincerely wonder who they might be if the trust did not exist—would they be happier, and would they hold their own unique abilities and gifts in higher esteem? In addition they feel beholden to someone they often will never meet, and scarcely even feel related to, yet whose history they are expected to appreciate, admire, and emulate. In fact they may be embarrassed by that history while being locked into it by the trust.

Yet another reality of trust life is nonmentoring trustees. Many trusts fail their founders' hopes that they will enhance the lives of their beneficiaries because the trustees of such trusts themselves go into entropy. Often trustees fail to change with the times and bring outdated thinking to new problems. Worse, some trustees begin to see themselves as the real owners of the trust's property, acting as if they are the founder's alter ego rather than the beneficiary's representative, and begin to believe they know better than the beneficiaries how the beneficiaries should live their lives. They arrogate to themselves the role of parents and, in the extreme, become autocrats, when properly their role is to serve the growth and development of the beneficiaries as human beings and as intellectual creatures. Too often, and especially in the later years of a long-lived trust, when the founder is long dead and successor trustees never knew him or her, the trustees begin to identify themselves and their stations in life by the trust's assets and start doing and acting accordingly, forgetting that they are the servants of the beneficiaries and of future generations of beneficiaries to come.

Thoughtful planners who suggest the formation of perpetual trusts and the founders who create them will realize that there is a heightened possibility of failed trust governance when the relationship between the beneficiaries and the trustee will last for an extended period of time. All trust governance is at risk of failure from the beneficiary's becoming remittance-addicted and the trustee's falling into entropy and self-dealing. Unfortunately, with a perpetual trust these risks are heightened, since there is simply more time for the law of entropy to work its will through the beneficiaries' and trustees' negative experiences of the trust and of their relationships with each other.

Happily, today enlightened advisers have an armamentarium of planning antidotes to protect beneficiaries and trustees against failed trust governance. Part Three of this book touched on many of them. One in particular is worth recalling here. As I discussed in chapters 10, 11, and 19, mentor-trustees working to create excellent relationships with their beneficiaries, and beneficiaries working to become excellent beneficiaries in managing their relationships with their trustees, have real possibilities of success. It is in the good management of these relationships that the trust's purpose has a reasonable prospect of being fulfilled. As the trustees and beneficiaries begin this process of self-government, what are some of the outcomes they might consider so that the trust, whether perpetual or fixed term, will provide the greatest enhancement to its beneficiaries' lives? I suggest that both parties begin by recognizing that for each beneficiary, the following three goals—(1) becoming fully self-aware and achieving personal freedom so as to be able to live an independent life, (2) achieving the fulfillment of his or her life's dreams through knowing and fulfilling his or her life's calling, and (3) being able to take full responsibility for his or her actions—are goals of high value and purpose. I worry that in a perpetual trust the beneficiaries may say, Why should I bother with becoming an excellent beneficiary and with trust governance, and do all the labor of making this relationship work, if neither I, nor my children, nor my future descendants will ever own the assets? Why should I learn to be a good steward? Why should I work, or be an apprentice, or find my calling, when I can do nothing?!

Who will help the beneficiary understand that these questions must be well answered if he or she is to achieve a full share of independence and self-worth? Let's hope that founders, alerted to these questions and realities by their planners, will both provide language within their trusts that raise these questions for their beneficiaries and select trustees prepared to help the beneficiaries find life-enhancing individual answers.

All trusts have the capacity to help beneficiaries become self-aware and independent, seek a calling, and be able to take full responsibility for their actions—or to empower them to do nothing and become dependent, with all the sadness such entropic lives engender. I am particularly concerned about perpetual trusts, however, because their history suggests they may have a greater risk of leading to dependence than fixed-term trusts. Whether my concerns will be borne out will be known only many decades from now, when the second and third generations of beneficiaries of such trusts take their places. It is my hope that this discussion and the questions it poses will offer today's trust planners and trust founders food for thought about the consequences their decisions may have on the lives of future beneficiaries. Perhaps the thought and time they invest in considering these questions will lead to their trusts' enhancing rather than diminishing those beneficiaries' lives. Should such a result be achieved by some perpetual trusts, it is likely that these trusts' founders will have taken Santayana's admonition about the past to heart.

Thoughtful giving begins with carefully considering whether a gift will do harm and then—after weighing its possibly harmful affects—whether it will do good.

Chapter Notes

1. This reflection originally appeared in somewhat different form in *The Chase Journal* (Volume 5, Issue 3, 2001).

2. The perpetual trust was also widely used by the Roman Catholic Church to hold its land, until in certain parts of England and France the Church became the largest landowner. As Europe's business environment modernized in the fifteenth and sixteenth centuries this fact caused much dissatisfaction with the Church's secular, rather than spiritual, role. The resulting stultification of commerce—land being its principal medium—was seen by the Tudors in England as highly prejudicial to England's development. As a result many people in the mercantile classes warmly welcomed as a necessary reform Henry VIII's decision as part of his Reformation to sequester and redistribute church property, because they saw its potential to accelerate the development of England's economy.

3. An excellent synopsis of the English legal history of this subject can be found in *Wills, Trusts and Estates*, Sixth Edition, by Jesse Dukeminier and Stanley M. Johenson (New York: Aspen Publishers, Inc., 1999).

4. I also wonder whether these planners have studied Aristotle's view of how difficult the journey is for Western man to be happy and how much of that journey is about knowing oneself, finding useful work in calling and living out one's own dream, and how little is about inheritance of other dreams as reflected by such monuments? Confucius, Socrates, the Buddha, Gandhi, and many twentieth-century figures like Jung, Maslow, and Erik Erikson also have much to say about this journey, and each in his own way comes to much the same conclusion about what enhances people's lives and what diminishes them.

EPILOGUE

I hope that as you have progressed through the chapters of this book, you have come to believe that it is possible for a family to achieve long-term wealth preservation. I am sure you also now realize how hard that is, and how relentless the forces implied by the proverb "Shirtsleeves to shirtsleeves in three generations" will be in trying to thwart your efforts. I also hope that the spiritual foundation on which your work as a family is predicated has grown along with your practices so that your experience of love, expressed as joy and gratitude for the blessings of your individual happiness and that of every member of your family, continues to sustain all of you now and into the future.

Together, we have learned that a family's wealth consists of three forms of capital—human, intellectual, and financial—and that the management of the first two is the most critical to the successful preservation of a family's wealth. We have discovered that this is an extremely long-term process, measured in periods of twenty, fifty, and one hundred years. We have determined that the mission of a family that decides to attempt long-term wealth preservation lies in enhancing the individual pursuits of happiness of each family member in order to promote growth of the human, intellectual, and financial assets of the family as a whole.

We have discussed practices that will help us achieve our goal, especially those we use to express and share what we have learned about ourselves and our families to benefit the outside world through philanthropy, which is our family's social capital. Above all, we have realized how courageous we have to be to embark on a family journey that will extend beyond our own lifetimes and thus be a journey whose outcome we will never know. To begin a voyage knowing we will not see its end is a leap of faith of extraordinary proportions. Yet not to try is to accept the verdict of the proverb and consign our families to fulfilling its hopeless prophecy.

In the Middle Ages, throughout Europe, when people felt a calling of faith they went on a pilgrimage. In France, the word for this journey of faith is *pèlerinage,* the journey of the peregrine falcon. That journey of faith began in Paris and followed a route through France, across the Pyrenees Mountains into Spain, and ultimately to the Shrine of Santiago de Compostela in the extreme northwest of Spain. Many of the pilgrims knew when they began the journey that it was unlikely, if not impossible, that they would survive the route. Courageously, they set out anyway.

In order that people along the route would know they were pilgrims, they wore and carried certain symbols of their act of faith. First, a scallop shell was worn around the neck, a symbol of Saint James, to whom the shrine at Compostela is dedicated. Next, a special round hat, and finally a special staff. By these three symbols, all who encountered them on the route knew them to be people of courage, committed to a journey based on faith.

This book was written to offer you a challenge, and a map, and a place from which to begin such a *pèlerinage.* I hope that you and each member of your family will join me on this extraordinary journey by putting a scallop shell around your neck, donning a round hat, picking up a staff, and starting the long walk to the successful preservation of your family's wealth. May every one of your journeys be successful.

BIBLIOGRAPHY

This bibliography is selective of those books I feel most informed the ideas in the book.

Aldrich, Nelson W. Jr. *Old Money: The Mythology of Wealth in America*. New York: Allworth Press, 1996.

Alighieri, Dante. *The Divine Comedy—Inferno*. Translated by John Ciardi. New York: Modern Library Edition, 1996.

Aristotle. *Nicomachean Ethics*. Translated by J. A. K. Thomson, revised by Hugh Tredennick. London: Penguin Books, 1953.

———. *The Politics*. Translated by T. A. Sinclair, revised by T. J. Saunders. London: Penguin Books, 1992.

Bergson, Henri. *Creative Evolution*. Toronto: Dover, 1998.

Blouin, Barbara, with Katherine Gibson and Margaret Kierstal. *The Legacy of Inherited Wealth*. U.S.: Triopress, 1995.

Boorstin, Daniel J. *The Discoverers*. New York: Vintage Books, 1985.

———. *The Creators*. New York: Vintage Books, 1993.

———. *The Seekers*. New York: Random House, 1999.

Bork, David, Dennis T. Jaffe, James H. Lane, Leslie Dashew, and Quentin G. Heisler. *Working with Family Businesses*. San Francisco: Jossey-Bass, 1996.

Bowen, Murray. *Family Therapy in Clinical Practice*. Northvale, NJ: Jason Aronson, Inc., 1985.

Bronfman, Joanie. *The Experience of Inherited Wealth: A Social Psychological Perspective*. Boston: UMI Dissertation Services, 1987.

Burke, Edmund. *Reflections on the Revolution in France*. London: Penguin Books, 1986.

Carloch, Randall S., and John L. Ward. *Strategic Planning for the*

Family Business. Hampshire, UK: Palgrave, 2001.

Carnegie, Andrew. *Gospel of Wealth.* Bedford, MA: Applewood Books Reprint, 1998.

Cavalli-Sforza, Luigi Luca. *Genes, Peoples and Languages.* New York: North Point Press, 2000.

Chaucer, Geoffrey. *The Canterbury Tales.* Oxford: Oxford University Press, 1998.

Chernow, Ron. *The House of Morgan.* New York: Simon & Schuster, 1990.

Cicero. *On Government.* Translated by Michael Grant. London: Penguin Books, 1993.

Collier, Charles W. *Wealth in Families.* Cambridge: Harvard University, 2001. Available from the University at 617-495-5040.

Comte-Sponville, Andre. *A Small Treatise on the Great Virtues.* New York: Metropolitan Books, 1996.

Confucius. *The Analects.* Translated with an introduction by D. C. Lau. Great Britain: Penguin Books, 1987.

Csikszentmihalyi, Mihaly. *Flow, The Psychology of Optimal Experience.* New York: HarperCollins, 1990.

———. *Creativity.* New York: Harper Collins, l996.

De Duve, Christian. *Vital Dust: Life as a Cosmic Imperative.* New York: Basic Books, 1995.

Diamond, Jared. *Guns, Germs, and Steel.* New York: W. W. Norton & Co., Inc., 1997.

Doud, Ernest A. Jr., and Lee Hausner. *Hats Off to You.* Los Angeles: Doud, Hausner and Associates, 2000.

Ehrlich, Paul R. *Human Natures.* Washington, DC: Island Press, 2000.

Elgin, Duane. *Awakening Earth.* New York: William Morrow and Company, 1993.

Ellis, Charles D. *Investment Policy—How to Win the Loser's Game.* Burr Ridge, IL: Irwin Professional Publishing, 1993.

Epictetus. *The Discovery of Epictetus.* Translated by Robin Hand. London: Everyman, J. M. Dent, 1995.

Esposito, Virginia. *Splendid Legacy: The Guide to Starting Your Family Foundation.* Washington, DC: The Center of Family

Philanthropy, 2002.

Foster, Steven, and Margaret Little. *The Four Shields: The Initiating Season of Human Nature*. Big Pine, CA: Lost Borders Press, 1998.

Friedman, Edwin H. *A Failure of Nerve*. Edited by Edward W. Beal and Margaret M. Treadwell. Bethesda, MD: The Edwin Friedman Estate/Trust, 1999.

Gardner, Howard. *Frames of Mind: The Theory of Multiple Intelligences*. New York: Basic Books, 1993.

Gersick, Kelin E., John A. Davis, Marion McCollom Hampton, and Ivan Lansberg. *Generation to Generation: Life Cycles of a Family Business*. Boston: Harvard Business School Press, 1997.

Gleick, James. *Chaos*. New York: Penguin Books, 1987.

Godfrey, Joline. *Raising Financially Fit Kids*. Berkeley: Ten Speed Press, 2003.

Goleman, Daniel. *Emotional Intelligence: Why It Can Matter More Than IQ*. New York: Bantam Books, 1997.

Gracian, Baltasar. *The Art of Worldly Wisdom*. Translated by Christopher Maurer. New York: Doubleday, 1992.

Greenleaf, Robert K. *Servant Leadership*. New York: Paulist Press, 1977.

Handy, Charles. *The Age of Paradox*. Boston: The Harvard University Press, 1995.

Harris, Judith Rich. *The Nurture Assumption*. New York: The Free Press, 1998.

Hausner, Lee. *Children of Paradise: Successful Parenting for Prosperous Families*. Los Angeles: Jeremy Tarcher, 1990.

Herz-Brown, Fredda. *Reweaving the Family Tapestry*. New York: W. W. Norton & Company, 1991.

Hillman, James. *The Force of Character*. New York: Random House, 1999.

Hoffman, Lynn. *Foundations of Family Therapy*. New York: Basic Books, 1981.

Huizinga, Johan. *Homo Ludens: A Study of the Play-Element in Culture*. Boston: The Beacon Press, 1971.

Jaynes, Julian. *The Origin of Consciousness in the Breakdown of the*

Bicameral Mind. Boston: Houghton Mifflin, 1990.

Johnson, Allan W., and Timothy Earle. *The Evolution of Human Societies*. Stanford: Stanford University Press, 1987.

Kauffman, Stuart. *At Home in the Universe: The Search for the Laws of Self-Organization and Complexity*. New York: Oxford University Press, 1995.

Kleberg, Sally. *Private Wealth*. New York: McGraw Hill, 1997.

Krishnamurti, J. *Education and the Significance of Life*. San Francisco: Harper Collins, 1981.

Lansberg, Ivan. *Succeeding Generations*. Boston: Harvard Business School Press, 1999.

Le Van, Gerald. *Lawyers, Lives Out of Control*. Alexander, NC: World Comm Press, 1993.

Linowitz, Sol, with Martin Mayer. *The Betrayed Profession*. New York: Charles Scribner and Sons, 1994.

Locke, John. *Two Treatises of Government*. London: Cambridge University Press, 1994.

Madison, James, Alexander Hamilton, and John Jay. *The Federalist Papers*. London: Penguin Books, 1987.

Montesquieu, Charles, Louis de Secondat, Baron de la Brede, et al. *The Spirit of the Laws*. Translated and edited by Anne M. Cohler, Basia Carolyn Miller, and Harold Samuel Stone. Cambridge, UK: Cambridge University Press, 1994.

Moore, Christopher W. *The Mediation Process, Second Edition*. San Francisco: Jossey-Bass, 1996.

Morris, Tom. *If Aristotle Ran General Motors*. New York: Henry Holt and Company, Inc., 1997.

Nanus, Burt. *Visionary Leadership*. San Francisco: Jossey-Bass, 1992.

Neubauer, Fred, and Alden G. Lank. *The Family Business: Its Governance for Sustainability*. New York: Routledge, 1998.

O'Neil, John R. *The Paradox of Success*. New York: Taracher/Putnam, 1993.

O'Neill, Jessie H. *The Golden Ghetto*. Center City, Minnesota: Hazelden, 1997.

Pascale, Richard T., Mark Milleman, and Linda Gioja. *Surfing the Edge of Chaos; The Laws of Nature and the New Laws of Business.* New York: Crown Business, 2000.

Peterfriend, Suzan, and Barbara Hauser. *Mommy, Are We Rich? Talking to Children About Money.* Rochester, MN: Mesatop Press, 2001.

The Philanthropic Institute. *The Philanthropic Curve.* Boston, 2000.

Pine, Joseph B., and James H. Gilmore. *The Experience Economy.* Boston: Harvard Business School Press, 1999.

Plato. *Timaeus and Critias.* Translated by Desmond Lee. London: Penguin Books, 1977.

———. *The Republic and Other Works.* Translated by B. Jowett. New York: Anchor Books, 1973.

Polybius. *The Rise of the Roman Empire.* Translated by Ian Scott-Kilvert. London: Penguin Books, 1979.

Prigogie, Ilya, and Stenges, Isabelle. *Order Out of Chaos.* New York: Bantam Press, 1984.

Rawls, John. *Justice as Fairness, a Restatement.* Cambridge, MA: Belknap Press of Harvard University Press, 2001.

Rue, Loyal. *By the Grace of Guile.* New York: Oxford University Press, 1994.

Santayana, George. *The Life of Reason (1905-1906), Volume I, Reason in Common Sense.*

Schon, Donald A. *The Reflective Practitioner.* New York: Basic Books, 1983.

Schwartz, Roger M. *The Skilled Facilitator.* San Francisco: Jossey-Bass, 1994.

Scott, Austin W. *The Law of Trusts,* Fourth Edition. New York: Aspen Publishers, Inc., 2000.

Smith, Huston. *The World's Religions.* New York: Harper Collins, 1991.

Sonnenfeld, Jeffrey. *The Hero's Farewell.* New York: Oxford University Press, 1988.

Sorokin, Pitirim. *Social and Cultural Dynamics.* Revised and abridged in one volume by the author. New Brunswick, NJ: Transaction Publishers, 1985.

Spengler, Oswald. *The Decline of the West*. An abridged edition by Helmut Werner, translated by Charles Francis Atkinson. London: Oxford University Press, 1991.

Stone, Deanne. *Building Family Unity Through Giving: The Story of the Namaste Foundation*. San Francisco: The Whitman Institute, 1992.

Sulloway, Frank J. *Born to Rebel*. New York: Pantheon Books, 1996.

Suzuki, Shunryu. *Zen Mind, Beginner's Mind*. New York: Wentherhill, 2000.

Tarnas, Richard. *The Passion of the Western Mind*. New York: Ballantine Books, 1991.

de Tocqueville, Alexis. *Democracy in America*. Translated by George Lawrence. New York: Harper Perennial, 1988.

Talbot, Michael. *The Holographic Universe*. New York: Harper Perennial, 1992.

Toynbee, Arnold S. *A Study of History*. Abridgement of Volumes I through X, in two volumes by D. C. Somervell. London: Oxford University Press, 1987.

Tzu, Lao. *Tao Te Ching*. Translated by Victor H. Mair. New York: Bantam Books, 1990.

Vaill, Peter B. *Learning as a Way of Being*. San Francisco: Jossey-Bass, Inc., 1996.

Van Gennep, Arnold. *The Rites of Passage*. Translated by Monica B. Vizdon and Gabrielle L. Caffee. Chicago: The University of Chicago Press, 1960.

Ward, John L. *Creating Effective Boards for Private Enterprises*. San Francisco: Jossey-Bass, 1991.

Wilber, Ken. *Sex, Ecology, Spirituality*. Boston: Shambala Publications, Inc., 1995.

———. *The Eye of Spirit*. Boston: Shambala Publications, Inc., 1997.

Wilson, Edward O. *Consilience: The Unity of Knowledge*. New York: Alfred A. Knopf, 1998.

Wolf, Fred Alan. *The Spiritual Universe*. New York: Simon & Schuster, 1996.

Wright, Robert. *The Moral Animal.* New York: Random House, 1994.

Zabel, William D. *The Rich Die Richer, and You Can Too.* New York: William Morrow & Company, 1995.

Zander, Alvin. *Making Boards Effective.* San Francisco: Jossey-Bass, 1993.

INDEX

adulthood, transition to, 52
advisers, 88, 93–94
Angus, Patricia M., 189
annual reports
    by family members, 60
    by family trustees, 60
Aristotle, 20, 23–24, 30, 208n4
assembly, family, 22–23, 173,
    175
asset(s)
    allocation, 64
    individuals as, 16
attorneys, xiii, 92–93
aunts, 52, 157–160

Bakal, Richard, 111
balance sheets, financial
    contents of, 57
    qualitative versus quantita-
        tive, 11
    time frames and, 9, 59
beneficiaries
    annual trustee's meeting,
        problems with, 104–105
    governance and, 106–107
    problems with, 103–107
    roles and responsibilities of,
        107–109
beneficiary/trustee relationship,

71–72, 111–113, 182,
    184–187, 206–207
    protectors, 85–87
    unexpected consequences,
        199–201
Bennis, Warren, 91
Bessemer Trust Co., 148
best friends, 90, 163
Beyer, Charlotte, 63
Bill of Rights, 23
Birla family, 35
birth, as a ritual, 53
boards of directors, 88
Bork, David, 46
Bowen, Murray, 73
Bronfman, Joanie, 70, 103
Buffett, Warren, 9, 63

Campbell, Joseph, 30
Canterbury Tales (Chaucer), xi
capital. *See* financial capital;
    human capital; intellec-
    tual capital; social capital
Carnegie, Andrew, 127
Carret, Philip, 9
Chaucer, Geoffrey, xi
*Children of Paradise: Successful
    Parenting for Prosperous
    Families* (Hausner), 46

About Bloomberg

BLOOMBERG L.P., founded in 1981, is a global information services, news, and media company. Headquartered in New York, the company has nine sales offices, two data centers, and 94 news bureaus worldwide.

Bloomberg, serving customers in 126 countries around the world, holds a unique position within the financial services industry by providing an unparalleled range of features in a single package, the BLOOMBERG PROFESSIONAL® service. By addressing the demand for investment performance and efficiency through an exceptional combination of information, analytic, electronic trading, and Straight Through Processing tools, Bloomberg has built a worldwide customer base of corporations, issuers, financial intermediaries, and institutional investors.

BLOOMBERG NEWS®, founded in 1990, provides stories and columns on business, general news, politics, and sports to leading newspapers and magazines throughout the world. BLOOMBERG TELEVISION®, a 24-hour business and financial news network, is produced and distributed globally in seven different languages. BLOOMBERG RADIO℠ is an international radio network anchored by flagship station Bloomberg® 1130 (WBBR-AM) in New York.

In addition to the BLOOMBERG PRESS® line of books, Bloomberg publishes *BLOOMBERG MARKETS*™ and *BLOOMBERG WEALTH MANAGER*®. To learn more about Bloomberg, call a sales representative at:

Frankfurt:	49-69-92041-0	São Paulo:	55-11-3048-4500
Hong Kong:	852-2977-6000	Singapore:	65-6212-1000
London:	44-20-7330-7500	Sydney:	61-2-9777-8600
New York:	1-212-318-2000	Tokyo:	81-3-3201-8900
San Francisco:	1-415-912-2960		

FOR IN-DEPTH MARKET INFORMATION AND NEWS, visit the Bloomberg website at www.bloomberg.com, which draws from the news and power of the BLOOMBERG PROFESSIONAL® service and Bloomberg's host of media products to provide high-quality news and information in multiple languages on stocks, bonds, currencies, and commodities.

About the Author

JAMES E. "JAY" HUGHES JR. is a sixth-generation counselor-at-law, now retired, and author of many influential articles, including a series of reflections on family governance issues and wealth preservation. He was the founder of the New York City law firm Hughes and Whitaker, where he focused on the representation of private clients throughout the world. He is renowned for facilitating multigenerational family meetings with an emphasis on mission statements and governance issues. In addition, Mr. Hughes has spoken frequently at numerous international and domestic symposia on estate and trust planning.

He is an emeritus member of the board of The Philanthropic Initiative, a counselor to the Family Office Exchange, an emeritus faculty member of the Institute for Private Investors, a retired member of the board of the Albert and Mary Lasker Foundation, and a senior dean of the Family Capital Institute (FCI). In addition, Mr. Hughes is an adviser to New Ventures in Philanthropy, a member of the boards of various private trust companies, and an adviser to numerous investment institutions. Educated at The Far Brook School, he is a graduate of The Pingry School, Princeton University, and the Columbia School of Law. He resides in Aspen, Colorado.

Readers may contact the author and learn more about his ideas at http://jamesehughes.com.